Love to Graham P. – Jack & Glenis

May 89

CW01648807

PICTURE PALACE TO SUPER CINEMA:

A HISTORY OF STOCKPORT'S CINEMAS

by

WILLIAM SHENTON

Metropolitan Borough of Stockport,
Leisure Services Division, 1988

© Stockport Metropolitan Borough

ISBN 0 905164 66 0

Printed by Deanprint Ltd.
Cheadle Heath Works,
Stockport, Cheshire SK3 0PR

CONTENTS

Introduction

In 1946 there were twenty-eight cinemas in Stockport and district. Forty years later only five of these have survived and, although they are well patronised, they can no longer be said to represent the most popular form of mass entertainment. They survive because there is no real alternative to seeing a film in a darkened auditorium, and no television—usually connected today by a co-axial umbilical to a V.T.R.—can hope to replace it. The "box" cannot compete in screen size or quality of picture, and in a cinema you are not disturbed by ringing telephones, or a spouse who wants to make tea. Nor are the "calls of nature" ever quite as compelling in a cinema! Unfortunately, cinemas that remain have lost their character, and the interiors of most of today's multi-screen cinemas seem to blend into one. Gone too is the sense of occasion that accompanied a night out at "the pictures". Seated in the darkened auditorium, lost in the feature film, the mundane real world outside seemed far away, at least for a couple of hours.

Almost a generation has passed since most of the district's cinemas closed during the 1950s and 1960s and, apart from the Cannon, Davenport, Regent, Savoy and Tatton, all have been progressively cut away before the electronic sythe of television. The process began with BBC television broadcasts to the North West in 1949, and gained momentum with the televising of the Coronation in 1953 and the opening of ITV in the area in 1956. After this latter event the local bus company reported a dramatic decline in the number of bus journeys made after 6.00 p.m. Later the introduction of colour television took away more of the big screen's advantage, and more recently the spread of the video tape recorder has hastened the cinema's decline. For half a century "going to the pictures" was the predominant form of popular entertainment, in spite of being despised by the academic and literary worlds, and over-censored by nervous politicians and frightened clerics. An echo of this popularity can be gauged from the number of old black and white movies (a "Yank" word) on TV, and I suspect that many older people are not so much watching Ginger Rogers and Fred Astaire, but remembering luxury nights out in the Art Deco splendour of the local super cinema. However partial and imaginary, the cinema did bring a wider world—especially through the newsreels—to a provincial and traditionally minded audience. For the many unemployed—when they could afford it—a 6d packet of "fags", and a night at the "flicks" did make a second-hand life somewhat more bearable.

Women, especially, enjoyed the advent of the local cinema, and for a while the films allowed them to escape from a world of long hours in the mill, few labour saving devices and childbearing. Previously, there had been church concerts, but how could you compare recitations to glamour fantasy? Older women, for example, often went to special mothers' matinees where they could get a cup of tea as part of the price of admission. They could legitimately get out of the house to a "respectable" environment, and enjoy themselves. Before the cinema their men-folk were almost equally restricted, but, for them, there was at least the outlet of football at Stockport County.

The cinema was also an essential part of growing up, and especially the Saturday

An Art Deco bas-relief mural in the Piaza cinema. This type of decoration was typical of the larger 1930s super cinemas.

Before cinemas were built local theatres were a regular venue for early film shows. The Grand Theatre had frequent displays as part of its variety programme. This theatre was pulled down in 1904, and the Hippodrome, later the Astor Cinema, was built on the site. The photograph shows the entrance to the theatre on St. Petersgate during the years 1901-02.

matinees. For children it was a vivid experience, if sometimes a little "red in tooth and claw" as one local author remembers:

> "Of course, we had the pictures, and Saturday mornings saw a queue outside the local "bug hut". We usually went to the Gem Picture House in Portwood because it was nearest. It cost one penny to go in, and they would also give you a comic and an orange. There were wooden forms at the front, and seats with a bit of plush at the back. I never really cared for the adventures of Pearl White & Co. because I could never see the screen properly—it was only in my adult days that I found I needed glasses. However, I did like the music played at the side of the screen by a piano lady. I only went because I had to take my brother, and everyone went to the pictures on Saturday mornings. If possible I sat on the back row against a five foot wooden boarding where late comers used to lean. If someone was behind your seat they kicked, and yanked your hair—my ringlets were pulled like bell ropes. Horrible boys spat at each other, or squirted oranges."

Another essential element in the popularity of the cinema was the great unmentionable—SEX! Not on the screen, of course, but among the audience. Concern was expressed as early as 1909 about the opportunities afforded for "improper conduct" by the darkened interiors of cinemas. Experiments followed with lighting systems, but soon ended when it was found that audiences preferred the darkness. Indeed the cinema owners offered further encouragement with plush double seats for courting couples; perhaps that is why producers got away with so many bad "quota quickies"—the audience was otherwise engaged. Marriages were sealed at the altar, but began on the back row of the stalls or balcony.

Many cinemas were never luxurious or "super", but built as "flea pits" or "bug huts". By the 1960s, after years of neglect, the dim lighting had a further purpose in some once grand cinemas, namely to hide the faded decorations and sagging seats. Perhaps we did not mind so much, or our standards were not so high, but it never, for me at least, spoilt the film. And that, of course, was why you were there. Nostalgia is usually a bad guide to the past, but when writing about the cinema, it is impossible to ignore.

W. Shenton
October 1987

Acknowledgements

I would like to thank the following individuals and organisations for providing information, material and advice. Without their help, and sustained interest, it would not have been possible to write this book. Stuart Bale, Commercial, Architectural and Shipping Photographer, of Liverpool, who took photographs of the Davenport, Plaza and Rota in the 1930s; John Cannon, of Cambridge, for permission to reproduce his photograph of Edgeley Pictures; Jack Edge, Chairman of the Tatton Group, Davenport Theatre; Mrs. Lynn Hamilton for her forbearance while my colleague, and editor, David Reid, upended the Local Studies Library in search of cinema material; Barbara Hampson and Jean Shawcross, for typing the original manuscript; Edith Hinson for quoting from her book *Mary Ann's Girl: Memories of Newbridge Lane,* (1984), p. 20; Mrs. Ros Lathbury who helped trace many prints in the photograph collection of the Local Studies Library; Messrs David and J. J. Lillis of the Regent Cinema, Stockport Road, Marple; J. T. L. Mallard, Bill Ball, Emily Hulme, Doreen Bradbury and Joyce Henry for their memories of local cinemas; Mr. Bert Minister for copying his drawing of the Queen's Cinema printed in *Portwood: A Collection of Memories,* (1982), p. 26; the North West Film Archive at Manchester Polytechnic, and particularly Maryann Gomes, Film Archivist, and Marion Hewitt, Assistant Archivist; Mr. Stan Parkinson for his skill as a photographer, and care in copying old and fragile material; Mr. Ian Statham; the staff at Stockport Reference Libary who, in the course of my researches, changed many microfilm reels for me in the Local Studies Library; and Mr. John D. Thompson, of Photo Graphic, Birkenhead, who allowed me to reproduce material from the Stuart Bale archive.

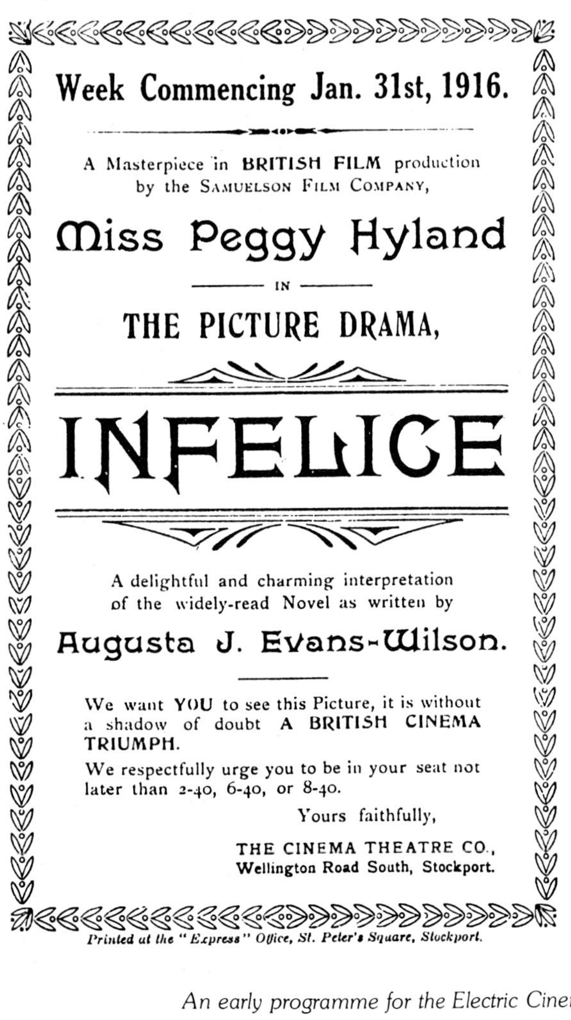

Week Commencing Jan. 31st, 1916.

A Masterpiece in BRITISH FILM production by the SAMUELSON FILM COMPANY,

Miss Peggy Hyland

IN

THE PICTURE DRAMA,

INFELICE

A delightful and charming interpretation of the widely-read Novel as written by

Augusta J. Evans-Wilson.

We want YOU to see this Picture, it is without a shadow of doubt A BRITISH CINEMA TRIUMPH.

We respectfully urge you to be in your seat not later than 2-40, 6-40, or 8-40.

Yours faithfully,

THE CINEMA THEATRE CO.,
Wellington Road South, Stockport.

Printed at the "Express" Office, St. Peter's Square, Stockport.

CINEMA THEATRE, WELLINGTON ROAD, STOCKPORT.

Calendar of CINEMA TRIUMPHS for February, 1916.

Commencing Monday, January 31st – For 6 Days only:

MISS PEGGY HYLAND

IN THE MASTERPIECE OF PICTURE DRAMA,

"INFELICE,"

A WONDERFUL ADAPTATION OF THE WIDELY-READ NOVEL BY

AUGUSTA J. EVANS-WILSON.

Commencing			Featuring
Feb. 7	—Three Days	"MISTRESS NELL"	Mary
„ 10	„	"HIS CRUCIBLE"	Edmund Cobb
„ 14	„	"RAGS"	Mary Pickford
„ 17	„	"CHARLIE SHANGHIED"	Charlie Chaplin
		"ACROSS THE BORDER"	Miss Grace McHugh
„ 21	„	"JIM, THE PENMAN"	John Mason
„ 24	„	"THE LADY OF THE SNOWS"	Edna Mayo Richard Travers
„ 28	„	"THE COMMANDING OFFICER"	Donald Crisp
Mar. 2	„	"THE SCAPEGOAT"	Miss Edna Mayo Bryant Washburn

CINEMA THEATRE FOR CINEMA TRIUMPHS.

ORCHESTRAL MUSIC. ACME OF COMFORT.

An early programme for the Electric Cinema Theatre, note Charlie Chaplin as one of the players.

A Brief History of the Cinema in Stockport

The building we know as a cinema was largely the creation of the Cinematograph Act of 1909. The main reason for the Act was the danger of fire associated with the use of highly inflammable nitrate film (which continued in use until the early 1950s). Local authorities would henceforth inspect premises before they were opened to ensure they conformed to the safety requirements of the Act. A licence, renewable annually, would then be issued permitting cinematograph exhibitions to take place. The local Watch Committee was the responsible body, and the first licences were issued in Stockport in January, 1910. Prior to this films were shown in the town as part of a variety bill in a theatre, or in halls or tents by travelling showmen.

The first recorded exhibition of films in Stockport was at the New Theatre Royal for the week commencing Monday, 29 June 1896. The theatre programme announced a dramatic presentation of *Trilby:* ". . . preceded each evening by the wonder of the age The Cinematographe—animated pictures, representing with marvellous accuracy scenes of everyday life!" A contemporary press report described the Cinematographe as "a machine whereby a series of photographs are thrown on the screen at the rate of 20 a second and following each other so closely they give life to the picture, and the photograph actually appears to be animated". The Lumiere Cinematographe had first been presented in Paris in March 1895, with the first British demonstration in February 1896 at the Polytechnic, Regent Street, London.

The nature of the films shown at the New Theatre Royal is not recorded, but it is probable that they were the same as those presented at the Free Trade Hall in Manchester some six weeks before. This short programme, shown at half-hourly intervals in Manchester, consisted of very brief scenes. The Manchester Guardian described them as follows: "One scene shows a number of factory girls issuing from the gates of a Lyons factory, with all the bustle and activity that mark departure at meal times. Bicyclists too, mount their machines and ride off through the laughing crowd. Other pictures are of a train arrival at a French country station, of card playing in a Paris cafe, and of domestic scenes".

Later that year the Grand Theatre of Varieties, during the week commencing 7 December, presented the "Famous

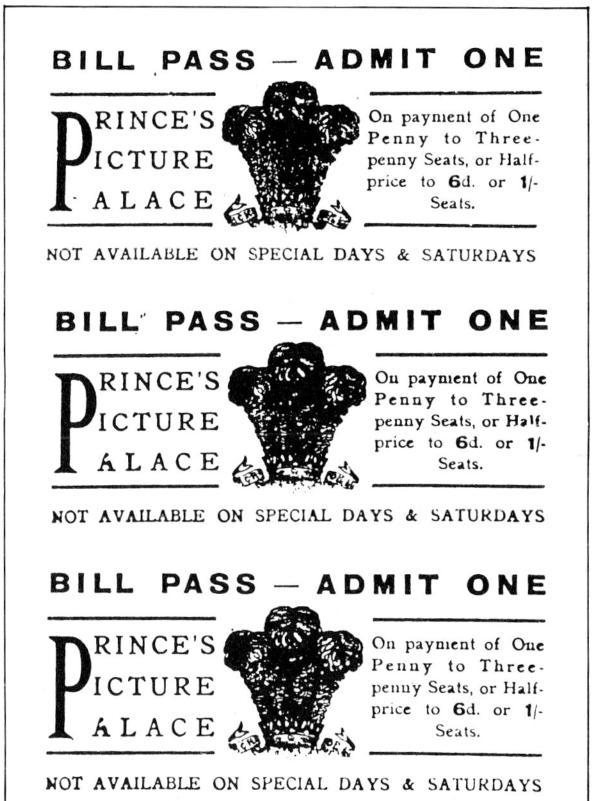
BILL PASS — ADMIT ONE

PRINCE'S PICTURE PALACE

On payment of One Penny to Threepenny Seats, or Half-price to 6d. or 1/- Seats.

NOT AVAILABLE ON SPECIAL DAYS & SATURDAYS

BILL PASS — ADMIT ONE

PRINCE'S PICTURE PALACE

On payment of One Penny to Threepenny Seats, or Half-price to 6d. or 1/- Seats.

NOT AVAILABLE ON SPECIAL DAYS & SATURDAYS

BILL PASS — ADMIT ONE

PRINCE'S PICTURE PALACE

On payment of One Penny to Threepenny Seats, or Half-price to 6d. or 1/- Seats.

NOT AVAILABLE ON SPECIAL DAYS & SATURDAYS

Cinema tickets used at the Prince's Picture Palace c. 1912-14.

Cinematograph, Edison's Wonder of the 19th Century", on a programme including "a number of talented variety artists". The films were changed each evening, and included: the coronation of the Czar of Russia; scenes of Bolton railway station; Jenny Mills, skirt dancer; a cock fight; Sandow, strongest man on Earth giving his show; breaking waves at Blackpool; the beheading of Mary, Queen of Scots; the burning of Joan of Arc at the stake; and a reproduction of that year's Derby.

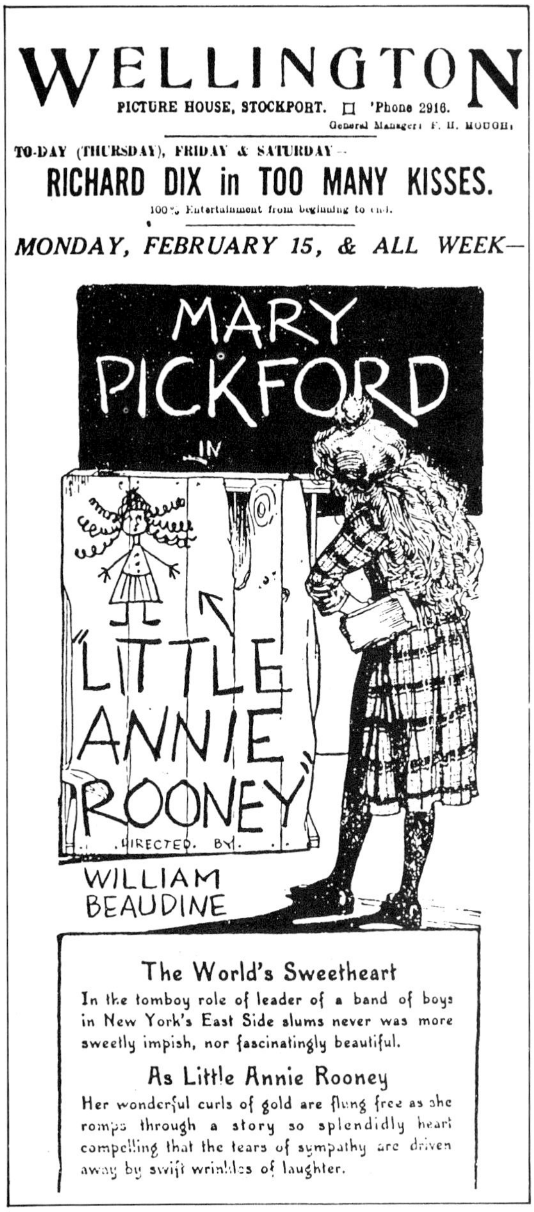

Cinema adverts for popular films of 1926 reproduced from Stockport newspapers.

Between 1897 and 1908, when the first regular performances began, a number of travelling companies presented films at many local venues, including the Armoury, the Grand and Empire theatres, the Mechanic's Institute and the Central Hall, Hillgate. In 1898 Tony Felix's Royal Imperial Circus visiting the Waterloo fairground site presented Professor Boscoe's Great Bon Fantiscope for a week, the Stenograph for a week and, due to its popular success, Watson's Cinematograph for three weeks. The Theatre Royal included the Phono-Bioscope in its programme during November 1901. This was an early talking picture apparatus, with films presenting music hall stars singing their principal songs, and included Vesta Tilley, Alec Hurley and Lil Hawthorn. Edison's Animated Pictures Company at the Mechanic's Institute in September 1901 offered films of local scenes including workers leaving Christy's hat factory on Hillgate, a ride on a new electric tram to Woodley and the turnout of the Stockport Fire Brigade. Ohmy's Circus visiting Portwood in October 1904 included a film of the laying of the foundation stone for the new Stockport Town Hall.

One local showman was Thomas Gould, a photographic dealer on Chestergate. He was well known in the town for operating lantern slides at lectures, and arranging limelighting for amateur theatrical groups. In November 1899 he gave a cinematograph entertainment in the National Schools, and the programme for St. Mary's Parish annual party held on Tuesday 18 November 1900, included the following note: "The entertainment after tea will be given by the choir, and will conclude with a cinematograph exhibition by Mr. T. Gould. Among the pictures shown will be naval gun crossing the Vet River drift; the fall of a chimney 150 feet high; the surrender of Kroonstad to Lord Roberts, and Off to the Front by armoured train between Belmont and Modder river in South Africa".

The first regular performances of films were offered at the Mechanics Institute, where the New Century Animated Pictures Company established itself in March 1908. This became the first premises to be licenced for full-time use as a cinema under the 1909 Act, and a licence was issued on 28 January 1910. At the same time the Empire Theatre was also granted a licence. In

April 1910 John Grundy, proprietor of the Star Skating Rink on Higher Hillgate, was granted a cinematograph licence for a cinema sited above his skating rink. The first purpose built cinema in the town was ceremonially opened by the Mayor as The Stockport Electric Theatre (later to become the Super-Cinema) in October of the same year.

These early licences only permitted cinemas to open between 2.00 p.m. and 10.30 p.m. and allowed: "no exhibition on Sundays, Good Friday, Christmas Day or any day appointed by the authority for public fast or humiliation". The programmes offered in the early days would consist of a number of short films, with a pianist providing musical accompaniment, and occasionally live acts appearing on the bill. Where only one projector was in use the manager would fill in with monologues or recitations while reels were changed, and would often provide commentaries for the films. Some of the pianists such as A. Brackshaw, resident pianist at the Star, Thomas Evans of the Edgeley, and Tom Burns, Jim Fantom and Fred Riseley of the Albert Hall, became local celebrities. As the industry grew films became longer, and the musical accompaniment grander, with some cinemas employing their own orchestra and providing elaborate musical preludes to the films.

In the early days European films, particularly those of the Frenchman Melies, were popular—they were billed at the Empire Theatre in November 1905—and immediately before the first world war both Italian and French epics enjoyed a vogue. However, the war gave dominance to the American film industry, and by the mid 1920s it has been estimated that almost 90% of the films shown in Britain were American. Despite government legislation on quotas for British films this dominance was to continue. The early films did not identify their actors, but from about 1910 film producers began to exploit the drawing power of star names, and included credits on films and publicity material. However, even before this audiences recognised performers, and christened them with names of their own invention.

The travelling showmen often changed their programmes nightly, but as exhibitions moved into permanent cinemas this evolved into twice-weekly, with exceptionally popular films being held for a week. With the introduction of talking pictures weekly changes became normal, but as the novelty wore off, twice weekly changes, and in the smaller local cinemas, thrice weekly changes became the norm.

As films played to packed houses in the town's cinemas, and stories circulated of the fortunes already made in the business, more local businessmen were tempted into the trade. Two new cinemas opened in 1911, a further two in 1912, and seven more in 1913. The number of licenced premises by the start of the First World War was seventeen, this included fourteen cinemas, two theatres (for short or occasional performances such as the presentation of D. W. Griffith's *The Birth of a Nation* at the Theatre Royal in December 1916) and the Centenary Hall of the Stockport Sunday School, which was licenced for occasional cinematograph shows.

In 1911 the Watch Committee stated that in future only ground floor premises would be licenced, and the following year prohibited the use of balconies. This latter ban was to remain in force until 1919 when the Don was granted permission to open it's balcony. During November 1912 the Stockport Theatre Proprietors Protection Association attempted to prevent further competition by asking the Watch Committee to use it's statutory powers, and refuse to licence any new cinemas. The committee was quick to point out that, as long as the premises complied with the requirements of the act, it was bound to issue a licence.

The cinema proprietors first applied to open on Christmas Day in 1914, but permission was refused. However, the following year permission was granted to open on Good Friday, providing each cinema applied individually, and submitted it's proposed programme for prior approval to the Chief Constable. From 1916 Christmas Day opening was also allowed with similar conditions. Despite many applications it was not until 1924 that the opening hours were extended to 10.45 p.m., and the following year to 11.00 p.m. Prior to this an individual cinema would have to apply for permission to open beyond 10.30 p.m., as it may need to if showing a particularly long film. In 1932 the hours were further extended by allowing opening from 1.00 p.m.

The influenza epidemic which followed the First World War led, in November 1918, to all cinemas in the town which gave continuous performances being closed to the public from 5.30 p.m. to 6.30 p.m. for thorough ventilation and spraying. Children under fourteen years of age were not to be admitted. A month later admission of children was permitted, and the closure limited to fifteen minutes.

The First World War depressed the cinema trade. Also the imposition of an Entertainment Tax in 1916, coupled with wartime shortages, made the business less attractive to newcomers. Consequently no new cinema was opened in Stockport until 1921. This was the Wellington, which was followed two years later by the Savoy on Heaton Moor Road: the latter was the last cinema to open in the town during the silent film era.

The 1909 Act gave local authorities an implicit right to censor films. The film distributors, to forestall official censorship, set up the British Board of Film Censors and gradually local councils came to accept the board's classifications. However, the local Watch Committee still had the right to authorise showings of films not granted a certificate. In 1929 the Stockport Watch Committee allowed exhibitions of *The White Slave Traffic*, but refused to allow *The Mysteries of Birth* to be shown. The gangster film *Scarface* was turned down twice, in 1938 and 1947, while the British scandal film of the 1940s, *No Orchids for Miss Blandish* was passed with only one scene, showing a man being kicked to death, removed. The committee achieved notoriety in 1954 by demanding cuts in Walt Disney's *Snow White and the Seven Dwarfs* before it could be screened as a U certificate film, and two years later banned *Rock Around the Clock* from the town's screens following reports of riots it had provoked around the country. In the 1950s the practice of local certificates became more common with the emergence of more adult films, and continued into the permissive 1960s.

The marvel of talking pictures arrived at the Alexandra Cinema on 3 August 1929, and over the next two years all the town's cinemas were fitted for sound. Silent films continued to be shown in some of the smaller cinemas well into 1931. In an attempt to compete with sound films, some cinemas not yet fitted for sound, would employ singers to sing along with the silent versions of *The Jazz Singer* and other early talkies. The end of silent films meant the end of regular employment for many local musicians employed in the town's cinema orchestras.

During the 1920s cinemas had become more elaborately designed and better constructed, but the 1930s was the age of the lavish and ornate Super Cinemas. The first to open in Stockport was the Plaza, which still dominates Mersey Square, in 1932. With 1873 seats it became the largest cinema in town. The Carlton (now the Cannon) followed in 1937 with 1750 seats, and the Ritz, the largest cinema ever to operate in a town, with 2343 seats on opening in 1938. The distinction of being the last cinema to be built in Stockport belonged to the Empress, on Manchester Road, which opened in 1939.

Four views of the interior of the Plaza in 1932. Showing the cafe, the auditorium, screen and ticket office. Note the elaborate gilded decoration.

The Cafe: Restaurants were frequent adjuncts to large cinemas.

The auditorium.

The screen, organ and orchestra pit.

Plaza ticket office.

In April 1938 the town's cinemas were threatened with closure by a strike. On 10 April the electrician's trade union held a meeting at the Royal Oak, Hillgate, to discuss their claim for a 48 hour week and a new wage agreement for cinema operators (projection staff). Although the Stockport employers agreed to the demands, apart from the 48 hour week in cases where it was impractical, a strike notice was issued which was due to expire on Easter Monday, 17 April. The strike lasted for several weeks in Manchester, but Stockport's cinemas continued to run normally. Only one chief operator went on strike and was replaced. Pickets appeared outside the Palladium and Carlton, but soon moved away when it became clear that the cinema queues were uninterested in their cause.

With the outbreak of the Second World War all places of entertainment were immediately closed, but cinemas in Stockport were allowed to reopen on Saturday, 9 September 1939. Manchester's cinemas remained closed for somewhat longer, and so the town's cinemas played to fuller houses than usual. However, public concern over air raids lead to a fall in attendances for a short time, but audiences soon returned. In 1940 the Watch Committee permitted cinemas to open at 10.00 a.m. on Saturday for children's matinees.

Stockport Express

FAMILY BALLOT

ON SUNDAY CINEMAS AND GAMES.

•

At the Stockport Borough Council Meeting on Wednesday, August 6, the proposals to approve the opening of Cinemas and Parks Recreational Facilities on Sundays were deferred for further consideration.

With the desire to obtain public opinion on this controversial matter the "Stockport Express" asks its readers to state their wishes in the accompanying Ballot Form as a guide to the Borough Council.

WHAT ARE **YOUR** VIEWS?

Cut here

FAMILY BALLOT FORM.

Are you in favour of

SUNDAY CINEMAS.

NAME	YES	NO

The Sunday cinema ballot form used by the Stockport Express to measure public opinion in 1946.

The first Sunday cinema queue on the 13 October 1946 at the Carlton cinema.

At the end of the war regular Sunday opening was still not allowed. The first request to do so had been made by the cinema proprietors in 1924, and in 1941 a deputation from the Stockport branch of the Cinematograph Exhibitors' Association approached Stockport Council to argue their case. In return for permission to open on Sunday £1000 per annum would be donated to a fund to be shared by local charities, but permission was refused. The audience for Sunday performances was clearly revealed by Red Cross Sunday which was held on 21 May, 1944. On that Sunday the town's cinemas were permitted to open, with all takings going to the Red Cross Prisoners of War Fund, and the Cinema Trade Benevolent Fund. The renters provided the films free of charge, with cinema staff donating their services. The shows were scheduled to start at 7.15 p.m. At 6.00 p.m. queues were forming at the three town centre cinemas to open, the Plaza, Carlton and Super, and by 7.30 p.m. all three had put up the house full signs. Full houses were also reported at the Edgeley, Alexandra, Star and Wellington. The following year a ballot was held in the town on the subject, and this recorded 14,546 votes in favour, with 6,287 votes against. The town's cinemas opened regularly on Sunday from 13 October 1946, with part of the takings being paid into a charity fund. However, opening was only permitted from 5.00 p.m. and, because of the reduced takings and increased labour costs of Sunday opening, it became normal practice to show older films which were available at a lower rental fee on Sundays. Complaints quickly followed about the quality of programmes offered.

Unlike the First World War the Second World War increased box office takings, and 1946 was the peak year for cinema attendances in Great Britain. However, changes in public taste, slum clearance and, particularly, the introduction of television broadcasts to the region in December 1949, soon led to a drop in audience levels. In 1949 3264 TV licences were issued in the town, and by 1954 this had reached 29,401; the following year the number was 31,520, and by 1959 the total had reached 54,523. The beginning of ITV transmissions in the area in May 1956 severely hit cinema attendances.

There were nineteen cinemas operating in the town in 1946, but by the end of 1961 eight remained, and by 1970 only four survived. The Prince's was the first to close in 1951. New processes such as Cinemascope, stereophonic sound and 3-D were introduced in an attempt to halt the decline, but to no avail. In fact the cost of installing new equipment, particularly for Cinemascope, contributed to the decline of the smaller cinemas. Three cinemas closed in 1956, one in 1957, two more in 1958, and a further one in 1959. In 1960 the Entertainment Tax was abolished, and the following year saw a reduction in the Sunday cinema levy. However, the closures continued, and a new enemy appeared; this was Bingo, which quickly took over a number of cinemas. The 1970s saw the twinning of the Essoldo (ex-Carlton), and a smaller auditorium opened at the Davenport. In 1982 the Ritz became the town's seventeenth cinema to close since the war. Today the three remaining cinemas, with their five screens, face a new threat from the video recorder. However, it seems that there remains some future for the local cinema, and the recent large audiences for *Star Wars*, *Indiana Jones* and *Ghostbusters* is clear proof of its appeal.

Projection equipment then and now.

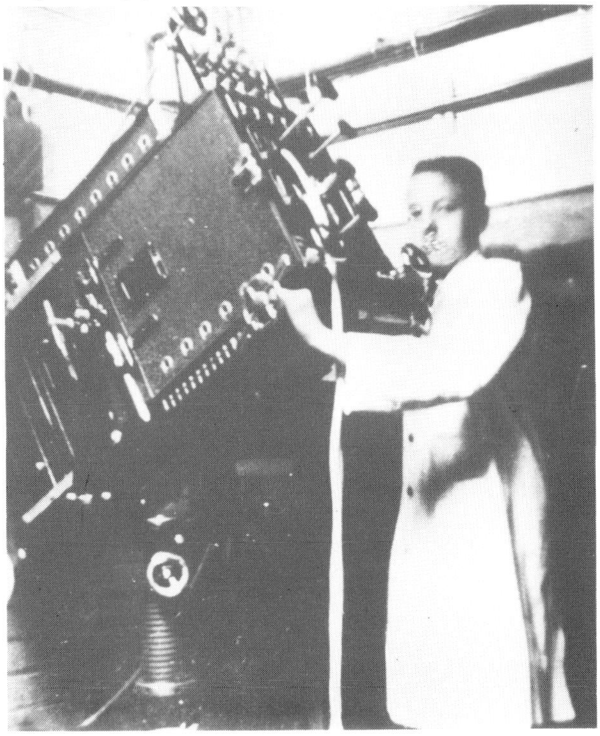

Savoy Cinema, Romiley, c. 1935.

Savoy Cinema, Heaton Moor, Projection Room 1986.

The Essoldo Cinema June 1971. View of the building after re-opening as a twin cinema.

List of Stockport's Cinemas

	Opened	Closed
Mechanic's Institute	1908	1911
Star	1910	1956
Electric Theatre/Cinema Theatre/Super-Cinema	1910	1965
Albert Hall	1911	1924
Prince's	1911	1951
Bijou	1911	1939
Gem/Queen's	1912	1940
Edgeley	1912	1956
Reddish Picture Hall/Pavilion/Embassy	1913	1933
Rota	1934	1959
The Picture House/Palladium	1913	1956
Don	1913	1957
King's	1913	1960
Brinksway Pictorium	1913	1958
Alexandra	1913	1961
Vernon	1913	1958
Wellington	1921	1963
Savoy	1923	Open
Hippodrome	1931	1940
as the Astor	1951	1960
Plaza	1932	1966
Curzon	1937	1960
Davenport	1937	Open
Carlton/Essoldo/Classic/Cannon	1937	Open
Ritz/ABC	1938	1982
County/Essoldo	1938	1969
Empress	1939	1959

Mechanic's Institute

The Mechanic's Institute was opened on 22 September 1862. The large hall, seating more than 1000 people, was used for various musical and dramatic performances, public meetings, lectures and dances. Films were shown there as early as 1897 as a part of Dyson's Diorama and Gypsy Choir Show, and between 1901 and 1903 the Edison Animated Pictures Company appeared a number of times. In 1905 the Parisian Animated Picture and Variety Company visited the hall, and the following year New York's Company presented 10,000 animated pictures.

Sydney Carter's New Century Pictures Company first played there for three weeks from Monday 26 September 1904. Prices were 1/-, 6d. and 3d., and they were to remain at this level throughout their visits. They paid return visits in June and August 1906; a further four were made during 1907, and they opened for a three week stay in February 1908. On 31 March 1908 the company opened for an advertised "short period only" and stayed until 16 April 1910. There was one performance nightly at 8.00 p.m., with a matinee on Saturday at 3.00 p.m.

Sydney Carter was born in Bradford in 1866. His father managed the St. George's Hall, and Sydney joined him at the age of thirteen. In 1898 he became manager, and introduced film shows in the following year. In 1902, in association with F. D. Sunderland, he formed the New Century Pictures Company. They began to tour film shows in 1903, and later ran halls in a number of locations including Leeds and Liverpool.

The early bills at the Mechanic's Institute also had live acts, and included singers, performing dogs and magicians. In September 1908 Gladys Cooper appeared and was billed as: "a serio and ballad vocalist". An early film programme consisted of *Monty's Motor, The Carnival, Pangs of Hunger* and *Dressmaker's Dummy*. Gaumont's Chronophone, an early talking picture apparatus, was first presented in August 1906, and made a number of popular return visits. One early sound film featured a rendition of the song When the Fields are White with Daisies.

The company also filmed local events to show as newsreels. A film of the Stockport Sunday School's procession was presented in June 1908, and also recorded was the visit of the Prince and Princess of Wales to open the new

Mechanic's Institute 1906.

Town Hall in July of the same year. From August 1908 the hall was billed as the New Century Picture Palace. In March 1909 a film of the Johnson vs. Burns fight of the previous December was shown at the special prices of 1s. 6d., 1s. 0d., 6d. and 3d., with three shows daily. In 1910, to comply with the new safety regulations, the projection apparatus was housed in an iron-sheeted box in the middle of the hall. The Franco-British Picture Company, based in Salford, took over from the New Century Company from 18 April 1910; it maintained the same prices, but gave two shows nightly at 7.00 p.m. and 9.00 p.m. The first programme consisted of the films *Pygmalion* and *Noel*, as well as contributions from the acting manager Ernest Percival, "the renowned London baritone". The Mechanic's Institute was scheduled to be pulled down to make way for the town's new central library, and the last performance took place on 16 September 1911. The building was demolished shortly afterwards.

PROGRAMME

MONDAY, June 26th, 1911, and during week.
ONE HOUSE NIGHTLY, INCLUDING SATURDAY.

Stockport Franco-British
Animated Picture Co.

One Performance Nightly, at 8.
MATINEES: MONDAY, 2-30; SATURDAY, 2-30.

APPOINTED MANUFACTURERS TO
H.M. THE KING, H.M. THE QUEEN, and H.R.H. THE PRINCE OF WALES.
A Choice Selection of
Fry's High-Class CHOCOLATES
Can be obtained from the Attendants.

SPECIAL NOTICE!

Every Monday at 2-30 o'clock, a Grand
FREE SPECIAL MATINEE
for all persons over 60 years of age.
Bank Holidays excepted.

ALL OTHERS USUAL PRICES.

PHENOMENAL SUCCESS OF "YOUNG CHARLIE."
FOR QUALITY AND LOW PRICES HAVE A LOOK AT ME. I NEVER FAIL TO PLEASE.
LEGS, 4½d. :: BEEF, 4½d. :: LAMB, 5½d.
NO. 1 STALL, MIDDLE AVENUE,
MARKET HALL, :: STOCKPORT.

NOTE.—If YOU are satisfied with our Entertainment: please recommend to your friends

MECHANICS' INSTITUTE, Stockport.

Manager : : : : Mr. FRANK H. VERNON.

Overture—"Royalty Waltz" *by Gladys Adamson*
Mr. Ernest Jones.

1. Stockholm (Topical).
2. Dairymaid and Sweetheart (Dramatic).
3. Lovemaking of Two Young Farmers (Comic).
4. Coronation Procession.
5. The Document (Dramatic).
6. Lobster Catching.
7. Fortune's Wheel (Dramatic).
8. Song—Selected
Frank H. Vernon.
9. Quiet Honeymoon (Comic).
10. Song of the Wildwood Flute (Dramatic).
11. My Wife's Birthday (Comic).

GOD SAVE THE KING.

This Programme is subject to slight alteration.

Remaining here until further notice.

Head Offices: BANK CHAMBERS, 3 Trafford Road, Salford.
Managing Director: Mr. WILBERFORCE TURNER.

ENTIRE CHANGE OF PICTURES WEEKLY.
EVERYTHING UP-TO-DATE

Cinema programme at the Mechanic's Institute 1911.

Star

The Star Picture Palace, on Higher Hillgate, was opened on 25 April 1910 by the local businessman John Grundy. The cinema was located on the first floor of the building; the ground floor being initially occupied by a roller skating rink, opened in the previous year, and also run by Grundy. Roller skating enjoyed considerable popularity at the time, and the town had a number of rinks. The premises had been opened in 1865 as an industrial school, before becoming Grundy's Mineral Water Manufactory about 1899. The opening programme offered *An Indian's Friendship*, *Eggs with Care* and "many more most comical pictures" at prices of 3d., 6d., and 9d. There was one show a night at 7.45 p.m., but Saturday had two shows at 7.30 p.m. and 9.00 p.m. There was also a special children's matinee on Saturday at 3.00 p.m. at prices of 1d. and 2d.

By August 1910 the cinema had proved so successful that it was closed for two weeks for extension, and the addition of a balcony and gallery. Later in the year it underwent further improvement. The popularity of roller skating declined, and in 1912 the cinema closed for four months to allow the building to be reconstructed into a single storey structure housing the cinema alone. The new cinema also included a balcony, but the Watch Committee refused permission for it's use. Despite many further applications, it was not until January 1924 that permission was finally granted to open the balcony to the public. The cinema as re-constructed seated about 700.

John Grundy died in November 1914, aged seventy-three, and the cinema was taken over briefly by Elijah C. Aspden, proprietor of the Edgeley cinema. Tom Isherwood, and his wife Annie, then ran the cinema until on Tom's death in April 1922, aged only thirty-three. Annie Isherwood continued to run the cinema alone. In 1928 control again passed to Elijah C. Aspden, who fitted sound equipment in 1930. A link with the cinema's past occurred in October 1935 when the manager, William Thornton Barlow, was bound over for twelve months by the local magistrates. He had forced open a doorway under the cinema which led into the warehouse of John Grundy Ltd. and, over a four week period, stolen forty-two bottles of Bass valued at 18s. 4½d. In 1937 Aspden sold his cinemas to the local Arderne cinema chain; this was taken over in 1948 by the Essoldo circuit, the final owners of the cinema.

On 7 January 1956 the Star was closed. An Essoldo spokesman blamed increases in wages and the rateable value, and linked the high rate of Entertainment Tax (40% of box office receipts) to the closure. Another factor was the shift of population away from the area in the post war rehousing programme; this had reduced the cinema's local audience on which it had come to rely. In 1960 a local car dealer requested permission to turn the building into a car auction room, but was refused. For some time it was used for the storage of motor vehicles, before being demolished in 1964. A petrol station was built on the site, and it is now in use by a firm hiring out gardening equipment.

Star Picture Palace January 1960.

Stockport Electric Theatre
Cinema Theatre
Super Cinema

On Wednesday, 12 October 1910, the Mayor of Stockport Alderman Arthur Briggs, officially opened the town's first purpose built cinema. The Stockport Electric Theatre, as it was first known, stood on Wellington Road South, opposite the present site of the Central Library. The builder, Josiah Briggs, was declared bankrupt in 1912 claiming to have lost £3000 on the contract to erect the Stockport Town Hall. The architect, G. S. Valentine of London, claimed this was the eighty-fourth picture palace he had designed.

The opening performance at 3.00 p.m. was for a specially invited audience, with the cinema opened to the public from 7.00 p.m. The first film shown was *The Mohawk's Way*, based on the Leatherstocking stories of James Fennimore Cooper. "Then the audience were shown how Muggy became a hero and they were very much amused by the hero's exploits. The modern prodigal series were intensely pathetic showing the career of a young man who leaves his home and old mother to make a fortune in the city. High-spirited and with the hope and courage of youth, he sets off determined to make his mark in the world. He returns an escaped convict and redeems himself by saving the life of a child. The last of the series was a love story and depicted how a lover by an act of folly, got himself into a serious scrape. Pictures of the Mayor and Mayoress thrown upon the screen were well received". Prices were 3d. and 6d., with reserved seats at 1s. 0d. Performances were continuous from 2.30 p.m., with afternoon tea being served free of charge from 2.30 p.m. to 5.00 p.m.

The original proprietors were The Stockport Developments Syndicate Ltd., with Frank H. Waters serving as manager until the end of the year when he was replaced by E. E. Allison. Early programmes featured "The Vivaphone—the wonderful pictures that sing and talk", and November saw the screening of "Special Stockport Pictures"; there were scenes of the mayor's procession, and of Stockport County's match against Burnley. In January 1911 the cinema presented a film of Gounod's *Faust:* ". . . beautifully coloured)—the full opera with orchestral accompaniment throughout—about 2000 feet of film, taking almost an hour to screen". In April plans were submitted to the Watch Committee for approval to construct a balcony, but permission was not forthcoming.

In September 1911 the cinema became known as the Cinema Theatre, and shortly afterwards the proprietors became The Stockport Public Hall Co. Ltd. (later known as the Cinema Theatre Company). E. E. Allison was replaced as manager by William H. Hague, who came from Sheffield in April 1912, and in December the licence was taken over by J. R. Charlesworth, a local accountant, who also held the licence for the Bijou cinema in Reddish.

J. H. Stansfield proprietor of the Prince's and Super Cinemas. The photograph was taken from a local election address dated October 1936. Stansfield was the councillor for Hollywood Ward.

Programmes were usually changed twice weekly, but in May 1912, Sarah Bernhardt, star of *The Lady of the Camelias*, was booked for a full week. On Saturday 4 January 1913 a special one day presentation was given of Kalem's *From the Manger to the Cross* at prices of 2s. 0d., 1s. 0d. and 6d., and in April that year the Italian spectacle *Quo Vadis*, "produced at a cost of $50,000", was shown at normal prices; this did such good business that it was held over for a second week. By the time D. W. Griffith's epic *Judith of Bethulia* was shown in November 1914, prices were 3d., 4d., 6d., 9d., with reserved seats still at 1s. 0d.

In May 1915, a short-lived policy of five programme changes per week was introduced; this included, "over 30,000 feet of cinematography weekly", accompanied by music, "in perfect harmony with the details of the productions". Under manager W. Asbery, and musical director Leon Hampson (later Madame Margaret Deane, or Mrs. Hampson), the orchestral music included pieces by Puccini, Boito and Tchaikovsky. Following the imposition of Entertainments Tax in 1916 admission prices were revised to 5d., 9d., 1s. 0d. and 1s. 3d.

Towards the end of the decade the cinema screened, amongst other films, two epics: Thomas Ince's *Civilization* (November 1917), and D. W. Griffith's *Intolerance* (January 1918). It regularly included Charlie Chaplin's films, a favourite in the town since 1914, in the programme. E. Broom became manager, and Thomas W. Evans, a well known local musician, musical director in 1919. Evans' involvement with cinemas had included a six year spell as pianist at the Edgeley; he later worked at the Grosvenor in Manchester, and at cinemas in Hazel Grove and Cheadle Hulme. He had also been a pianist at the Cinema Theatre before being appointed musical director.

The cinema was closed for a week in May 1919 for redecoration, and in October the following year the cheapest price for seats was dropped; the cinema now charged 9d., 1s. 0d. and 1s. 3d. E. J. Lyons was appointed manager in May 1921, and a few weeks later, on 18 June, the cinema was closed. It had been taken over by Stockport Palace Ltd., proprietors of the Princes cinema. The company was to retain ownership, apart from a period in the 1940s, when it was run by Hursthead Estates; and managed from no. 1 Lord Street, close to the cinema, until closure. The licence was taken over by Harrop Marshall, another local accountant, secretary of the company. The company's managing director, James Hampson Stansfield, was a town councillor and later alderman, and was well known for his interest in local sports, being, amongst other involvements, a director of Stockport County for some years. As a member of the Watch Committee he would frequently absent himself from committee proceedings when his cinema business was under review.

After redecoration, reseating and alterations, supervised by architect William Swann who had designed the Princes cinema for the company, the cinema reopened on Monday 29 August 1921 renamed The Super-Cinema. The orchestra had been "augmented", and the cinema was advertised as "the house that is perfect in detail". Prices at 1s. 3d. and 9d. were the same as those charged at the Prince's cinema.

Management of both cinemas was handled by Stanley Bridcut during the early 1920s, with the assistance of the young John F. Tatton from 1924. January 1930 saw the cinema advertising its programme as, "silent but sound entertainment", but on Monday 17 March of that year, the first talking picture programme was presented. It featured Maurice Chevalier in *Innocents of Paris*, two short films *Boyhood Days* and *Now and Then*, and the British Movietone News. Prices were now 4d. and 6d. for matinee performances, and 6d., 8d. and 1s. 3d. for evenings. During the early 1930s Stanley Bridcut became manager of the Prince's, and John Tatton took over at the Super. Following Harrop Marshall's death in 1932, J. H. Stansfield took over the licences for both cinemas.

In 1936 the Super became the town's first cinema to employ a pageboy; this was Bill Ball, then 14½ years of age. Shortly afterwards the new Plaza super cinema followed suit, but only for a brief period. As the Super had no sales kiosk, Bill Ball would obtain cigarettes and confectionery for patrons from a nearby shop. Tips supplemented his pay of 7s. 6d. per week, but the cigarettes he received in this way started him on a life-time's habit. His day would start at 10.00 a.m. cleaning the brasses, and assisting the doorman with posters. Later, after lunch, and starting with the matinee, he would open the cinema's inner doors for patrons and act as relief for the usherettes. He finished work at about 9.30 p.m.

The staff then consisted of the manager, four usherettes, two cleaners, a paybox attendant, a doorman, a pageboy and three operators (projection staff). Performances were now continuously from 2.00 p.m. to 10.30 p.m., with three separate shows on Saturday at 2.00 p.m., 6.30 p.m. and 8.40 p.m. The Saturday night performances were invariably full, with long queues waiting for uncollected booked tickets.

The cinema was again closed on 3 April 1937 for "complete modernisation". The front of the building was rebuilt, and extended to the side, thus providing a new foyer. A "balconette" was added at the rear of the auditorium, consisting of seats on a floor rising at a 45% angle. The cinema was also redecorated, reseated and the sound system was replaced with up-to-date Western Electric Mirrorphonic equipment. The seating capacity was increased by 350 seats to around 1000. The architect responsible for the modernisation was George Clayton, of Poynton, who had also designed the Tudor cinema in Bramhall. A car park had already been added in 1934 at the rear of the cinema; this area, known as Blue Shop Yard, was surrounded by tailors' workshops. The reopening, on Monday 4 October 1937, presented Shirley Temple in *Stowaway* and Clapham and Dwyer in *Variety Hour*.

A fire at the cinema on Sunday 20 March 1938 caused considerable damage to the stage, and the cinema was again closed. It reopened on

The Super Cinema January 1961.

4 July with the addition of a cafeteria built under the balconette, and accessed from the foyer and the front of the building; there were facilities for the purchase of sweets and cigarettes. After the fire Bill Ball became the cinema's third operator; he remembers racing to the Prince's with the shared newsreel, and then returning it for later showing at the Super. Films were stored in a fire proof safe, and any damaged pieces that were cut out of reels were destroyed in the cinema's boiler.

From 1940 John Tatton held the licences for the two cinemas until he left the company in September 1949. At the age of forty one, after twenty five years association with the Super, he gained the position of booking manager with a company controlling a number of cinemas and live theatres based in Sheffield. The licences were once again taken over by J. H. Stansfield until the Prince's closed in 1951, and the Super licence passed to W. R. Stansfield, one of his four sons, in January 1955. Harry Johnson became the cinema's manager in the 1950s.

During the 1950s the standard of the Super's programmes deteriorated, and consisted largely of reissues and the first showings of B films. By 1957 the nearby Essoldo was charging 2s. 0d. for front stalls and 3s. 6d. for the front circle, but the Super's highest price was 1s. 9d. During the late 1950s and early 1960s I remember seeing many older films, but the prints were well worn, with frequent jumps where damaged sections had been cut out. In 1962 planning permission was granted to redevelop the site as shops and offices, but this project was not pursued. James H. Stansfield died, aged eighty eight, in March 1965, and in October of that year the company applied for planning permission to turn the cinema into an entertainment centre to present wrestling, variety, club activities and bingo. Permission was not granted because of likely traffic and parking problems on the main road.

The cinema was finally closed on 27 November 1965, and the final programme was the Beatles film *Help* and *The Cool Mikado*. Admission prices were then 2s. 6d., 3s. 0d. and 3s. 6d. W. R. Stansfield blamed the closure on: "the difficulty of obtaining films which have not already had a showing in the town". In 1966 the building was put up for auction, but withdrawn when it failed to meet the reserve price of £45,000. It stood empty until purchased by the Crown Agents in March 1967 as the site for the town's new main post office. The Super cinema was demolished soon after.

Albert Hall

When it became clear that the Mechanic's Institute was to close, new premises were found just around the corner at the Albert Hall, on Wellington Street, opposite Lawrence Street. A cinematograph licence was first issued in December 1910, but the Franco British company did not open the cinema until 22 May 1911. This, the company's second cinema in the town, was under "the personal management of Mr. William Lovell Hurt" the licensee, with Sam E. Travis serving as acting manager and compere. The cinema appears to have been closed after a few weeks, but was re-opened on 18 September 1911 when the main company, now known as Stockport Animated Pictures, removed from the Mechanic's Institute. Prices were 9d. 6d. and 3d. Their first programme included the Gaumont film of Burgess swimming the channel, and the second week offered, "by special request": Uncle Tom's Cabin (in three parts), Man's Diplomacy (a real masterpiece), "New films in Western Subjects" and contributions by Harry Clegg the resident manager cum comedian. Originally the gallery was used by the public, although limited to seating for forty three people, but was closed by order of the Watch Committee in May 1913; it was then used only by the management and the pianist.

The building was opened in 1841, as a meeting room and Hall of Science by the Owenite socialists; it then became a spiritualist centre, and was named the Lyceum in 1848. Later it was used as a headquarters by the Oddfellows, and in 1895 it became the Albert Music Hall. By 1911 the ground floor was in use as a billiard hall with the first floor, formerly a roller skating rink, being converted into a cinema.

Wilberforce Turner, who had run the shows at the Mechanic's Institute, initially moved over to the Albert Hall, but Robert Allcock took over in August 1912; he was replaced in 1915 by Walter Charlesworth who also ran the Gem cinema. The final proprietors, from October 1921, were the Manchester and District Picture House Company Ltd.; this group also ran the King's Cinema.

The children's matinee was known as the "Saturday crush", and the reason is illustrated by the following incident. On the afternoon of Saturday 27 March 1912 the police visited the cinema, and found 884 children in the hall with seating for 480, and seventy six in the gallery with seating for forty three. The manager, in mitigation, said they were mostly poor children, and he didn't like to refuse them admission, but, he added, if he had refused they would have gone elsewhere. The record showed that 825 had paid 1d., fifty one had paid 2d. and eight had paid 3d. The proprietor was fined £10, plus costs, for not keeping the gangway, staircase and passages leading to the exits clear of obstruction; and £30, plus costs, for contravening the Children's Act, and not keeping stationed a sufficient number of trained adult attendants to direct the movements of the children.

On 21 March 1924 a portion of the ceiling collapsed during the night, and an inspection of the hall led to the cinematograph licence being revoked. However, the company was in financial difficulties, and it never reopened as a cinema. The first floor later became Bradley's Academy of Dancing, and continued as such for over thirty years. The ground floor has been a bookmakers since 1961, and the first floor is now offices.

The Albert Hall c. 1958. The first floor was used as a cinema.

Prince's

Thursday 26 October 1911 saw the grand opening of the Prince's Picture Palace, the first of two cinemas to be located on Prince's Street. The opening programme consisted of *Diamond Smugglers*, *Bess of the Forest* and *His Misjudgement*, promised the Palace News Gazette daily and musical selections played by the Palace Orchestra. In addition afternoon tea was served free to all parts. The cinema, which seated about 500, was designed by local architect William Swann for the Stockport Palace Ltd. The company retained control, apart from a period in the 1940s when the cinema was run by Hursthead Estates, until closure. The first manager was Frank H. Vernon who had held a similar position at the Mechanic's Institute. Prices were 3d., 6d. and 1s. 0d.

After the takeover of the Super cinema by the company in 1920 the two cinemas often showed the same programme, and both shared the same newsreels. Stanley Bridcut became manager in 1922. He had previously been a theatre manager in Preston, prior to which he had appeared for a time on the stage. When in Stockport he married Miss Mabel Cross of Edgeley. He left the town in 1939 to manage the Empire and Hippodrome cinemas

The Prince's Cinema January 1924. "If Winter Comes" was one of the most popular films of the year.

in Chorley. Bridcut died suddenly in December 1943, aged fifty seven.

In April 1929 the cinema presented the silent version of *The Jazz Singer*, with the: "special engagement of Fred Shaw—Al Jolson the second—who will render the following popular numbers during the evening performance—Sonny Boy, My Mammy, Dirty Hands, Dirty Face and There's a Rainbow Round My Shoulder". Talking pictures were introduced on 19 May 1930, the first talkie to be shown being *The Movietone Follies*, an all star revue.

In the late 1930s after the modernisation and expansion of the Super cinema, the Prince's became very much the poor relation. Its site, squeezed between shops, left no room for expansion. However, there were some modernisations in 1939. From the time Stanley Bridcut left, the cinema appears to have been managed from the Super, with the day-to-day running carried out by the chief usherette or cashier. After the war smaller older cinemas such as the Prince's were under a great deal of pressure. The box office takings generated by the Prince's seating capacity left it in an uncompetitive position compared with the grander and larger town centre cinemas. As a result the standard of programming declined, and consisted largely of reissues, first showings of B films and the showing of newer A films long after they had been seen at other town cinemas.

Closure came on 6 January 1951. The final programme was made up of a twelve year old Bing Crosby film *East Side of Heaven*, a *Three Stooges* short and a newsreel. The building was sold to the retail tailor chain of Montague Burton, who submitted plans for redevelopment of the site to the local council. The cinema disappeared in the re-building of the site in 1955, and included in the changes was the addition of a first floor. The building re-opened in 1956 as a furniture store.

Bijou

Reddish's first cinema was opened in October 1911. It stood on the corner of Gorton Road and Priory Lane, opposite what is now the County Bingo Hall. The original owners were the Reddish Electric Bijou Company Ltd. It appears to have been one of the many hastily and cheaply built structures thrown up to cash in on the cinema boom. This is confirmed by Stockport Town Council's conditional approval of the building to architects Ginger, Lee and Co., that the period in which it should remain erected was not to exceed five years. Largely constructed of wood and tin sheeting, with wooden benches in place of seats at the front of the hall, it seated about 500. This type of cinema, known as a "flea pit" or "bug hut", would be run as cheaply as possible.

One account describes the children's matinees in the silent days as mainly occasions for harrasing the manager, who appears to have run the cinema virtually single-handed, with occasional help from the pianist. The price of admission was 1d. and included a free comic. Another patron remembers that: "the piano accompaniment was provided by a Mr. Lea, who was a music teacher, and lived nearby. Sometimes there was a singer who often "stood in" when the film broke down. It was self-contained, and provided it's own electricity by means of a small gas engine supplied by the local firm of Richard Hornsby and Sons Ltd." A football team called the Bijou Athletic was run from the cinema; it was top of the second division of the Stockport Combination League in 1926.

In 1930 Frank G. Donaldson, who ran a cinema sound equipment firm in Manchester, took over the cinema, installed sound equipment and made other modest improvements. After the erection of a veranda at the front of the building in 1932, the name was changed to the New Bijou. The final owners, from February 1937, were Jackson and Newport (Reddish) Ltd. This company, which included Frank Donaldson as a director, opened the larger more modern County cinema next door in 1938. The Bijou was closed in July 1939.

For some years the building was used as a garage and car repair shop, before being demolished in 1968. The site was then cleared, and used for the sale of cars. It has since been grassed over, and is now fenced off.

The Bijou Cinema, Reddish, June 1966.

Gem, Queen's

Drawing of the Queen's Cinema by Bert Minister. Unfortunately, no photograph of this building has survived.

The first cinematograph licence in respect of the Gem Picture Palace, on Avenue Street, off Great Portwood Street, was granted on 12 January 1912. On opening, there was one performance each evening at 7.45 p.m., with matinees at 2.30 p.m. on Saturday (for children) and Monday (known as mother's matinee) and the programme changed twice weekly. This was another small cheaply run cinema like the Bijou, with a large part of its seating, for less than 500, on forms. It was, however, too close to the town centre to attract large crowds, relying on the less affluent members of the local community for its audience.

The cinema had a large number of proprietors. The original licencee was John W. West, who, in association with Thomas Baines of Middleton, ran the cinema until 1915, when it was taken over by Walter Charlesworth. It was then run by him in conjunction with the Albert Hall (and for a short period the King's) until 1918, when control of the cinema passed to the Gem Picture House (Stockport) Ltd., a company based in Bolton. In January 1919 Arthur E. Orton took over the management of the cinema, and in April the name was changed to the Queen's. There were two further licencees between 1920 and 1922, but from 1922 to 1932 it was managed and owned by Willis Popple. Probably the last of the town's cinemas to convert to sound, it had two more proprietors between 1932 and 1934.

The cinema first closed on 6 October 1934, when it was let to a Mr. Clarke of Stockport as a boxing hall. This was not a success, and the cinema reopened, after some alteration, under the "personal supervision" of Gordon Ray (he also ran the Brinksway Pictorium) as the New Queen's Cinema on Monday 1 April 1935. The opening programme was a British production, *The Red Wagon*, with American stars Charles Bickford and Raquel Torres; the film was supported by variety acts. "Uncle Gordon Never Fails", the advertisements proclaimed, but the cinema soon closed once again. It reopened on 16 September 1935 under new management, and the licence was held by Albert Mitchell. Relying on older films available at lower rental fees, the cinema was badly hit by the opening of the nearby town centre super cinemas.

The final proprietor, George Henry Turner of Bolton, took control in November 1938. He fitted a neon sign to the corner of the building. The cinema was finally closed in early 1940. In July 1940 Turner was fined at the Stockport Police Court for failing to pay National Health and Unemployment Insurance contributions for some of his staff in February of that year. In a letter to the court he claimed to have lost all his money in running the cinema.

The building then stood empty until being put to use by The Cornbrook Chemical Company as a warehouse early in 1945. The company effected some alterations in 1949, and at the time of writing the building, much changed, is partly used as a car repair shop (the old entrance hall) and partly by a printing firm (the old auditorium).

Edgeley

The Edgeley, Castle Street's first cinema, opened on 2 December 1912. It was built for local businessman Elijah Crompton Aspden, who ran it until 1937. Aspden had started his business career as a cab proprietor in Levenshulme, before joining his father's fishmongers business there. He later ran shops in Cheadle and Edgeley, and traded on Shudehill market. At one time he unsuccessfully stood as the Conservative Party candidate for the Shaw Heath ward of the local council.

Perhaps the standards of some early shows can be gauged by the Edgeley's opening claim of: "brilliant, flickerless and rock-steady photoplays". Prices were 2d., 4d., 6d., and 9d. with increased prices of 3d, 6d. and 1s. 0d. for Saturdays and holidays. The cinema seated about 700, but did not have a balcony. In 1937 Elijah Aspden sold his cinemas (he also controlled the Star) to Arderne Cinemas. He died on September 3 the following year aged sixty two.

Arderne Cinemas were taken over by the Essoldo group in 1948. The Edgeley was closed on 1 December 1956. Two and a half years later on 23 June 1959 a Woolworth store opened on the site, and is now in use as a freezer centre.

Interior views of the Edgeley Cinema c. 1930.

Reddish Picture Hall
Pavilion
Embassy

The second cinema to serve Reddish was on Gorton Road, adjoining the Bull's Head Hotel. It opened in April 1913 as the Reddish Picture Hall, with seating for 650. The first licencee was Harold E. Buxton, and in view of the later fate of the cinema, it is perhaps apt that the issuing of a cinematograph licence was delayed for a month until a direct link to the local fire station could be fitted. The original proprietors were the Reddish Picture Hall Co. Ltd., later becoming, until 1921, Reddish Pictures Ltd. The cinema's name appears to have been changed to the Pavilion around 1917. The cinema was a better standard of building than the Bijou, and regarded as a much more respectable establishment by its patrons. One such patron remembers the red coated doorman/commissionaire who stood at the cinema entrance. For a time in the 1920s it became part of J. F. Emery's circuit based at the Theatre Royal in Manchester, until Benjamin Parry took over in 1926. He ran the cinema, installing sound equipment in 1929, until early in 1932, when it was taken over by Jackson and Newport (Lancs.) Ltd., who changed its name to the Embassy.

The cinema's last performances took place on Friday, 8 December 1933. The film shown, *So This Is Africa,* starred Wheeler and Woolsey. The following day at about 2.00 p.m. a fire was discovered at the screen end of the building, and by 3.00 p.m. it had gutted the building, leaving only the frontage remaining standing. Luckily no matinee had been scheduled (they were held on Tuesday and Thursday) and no one was seriously injured. The manager Cyril Teal was attending Stockport County's cup tie with Crystal Palace at the time of the fire. The site is now occupied by shops.

Rota

The owners built a new cinema called the Rota around the corner from the site of the Embassy, and just over the Denton border. Although not in Stockport the cinema served the same area as the Embassy, and was usually advertised under Reddish. It was formally opened, exactly a year after the fire, on Saturday, 8 December 1934, with the first film performance on the following Monday. Designed by architect Henry Elder, a partner in the firm of Roberts and Wood, the cinema seated 820 in the stalls and 386 in the circle. Cyril Teal returned as manager from the company's Picturedrome cinema in Stretford. The Rota was taken over in 1936 by the national Union Cinemas circuit, which was merged into Associated British Cinemas in late 1937. It continued to be operated by ABC until it was closed in October 1959. The cinema was demolished in the 1960s and the site is now occupied by houses.

The Rota Cinema, Denton, December 1934. Although this cinema was just outside Reddish it was largely patronised by local people.

Picture House
Palladium

The town centre's largest and most lavish cinema of the silent era opened on 2 June 1913; it was built on the site of the Borough Carriage Company's old stables. The Picture House, on Prince's Street, was designed by Manchester architect Charles Swain and was run by Stockport Picturedrome Ltd. The cinema was built by Harold Brooke, who also owned the confectionery shop next door. His grandfather had been the founder of the Borough Carriage Company, and his father had run the Cafe Cecil on Prince's Street for many years. Harold Brooke later became a director of the Arderne company, which built the Carlton cinema. He died in August 1957, aged seventy six.

The Picture House, later the Palladium, Prince's Street, c. 1913.

The cinema offered accommodation for 1100 persons on tip-up seats, and boasted of, "orchestral music with original effects", from the theatre orchestra under the direction of Mr. R. V. Clarke. The opening programme offered a number of films including the dramatic *The Phantom Ship*, and the comic *The Stenographer's Troubles*. The first manager was Frank H. Vernon, late of the Mechanic's Institute and the Prince's, who often supplied monologues to supplement the programme. Prices were 9d., 6d. and 3d.

E. E. Allison, from the Cinema Theatre, became manager in 1915, to be followed by Harry Battersby the following year. The cinema's name was changed to the Palladium in February 1918. It was now run from the Palladium in Oldham, with Alfred M. Loader acting as General Manager. Prices were revised to 4d., 8d., 1s. 0d. and 1s. 2d., but the lowest price was dropped the following month. Attractions included Mary Pickford in *Such a Little Queen* (April 1915), *The Crisis* by Winston Churchill (December 1915) and the first Tarzan film *Tarzan of the Apes*, with Elmo Lincoln in the title role (January 1920).

The cinema's golden days began in 1922 with the appointment of Walter Bernice "Wally" Baker as general manager. He had started at the cinema in 1917 while still in his teens, and was promoted to the position of resident manager in 1920 under general

Cinema workers' trip to Blackpool August 1924. The man in the centre of the group of three in the middle of the photograph is "Wally" Baker, general manager of the Palladium.

manager Alfred M. Loader. The advertisements promised, "Pictures that please, music that matters", and claimed: "There is none better than the best, but there's one better than the rest". The theatre orchestra was billed as Baker's Rainbow Orchestra; it later became the Radio Orchestra, following the introduction of radio in the mid 1920s. In 1923 Wally Baker obtained extended opening hours to accommodate screening of D. W. Griffith's *Way Down East* starring Lillian Gish, and *The Four Horsemen of the Apocalypse* with Rudolph Valentino. In the same year he became known for the elaborate musical preludes he created, beginning with an Eastern Prayer Dance presented before the screening of *The Sheik*. In the following year he became the first of the town's cinema managers to apply for permission to open on Sunday. The Palladium was the first town centre cinema to install sound equipment, and opened its first talking picture, MGM's *The Broadway Melody*, on 14 October 1929.

"Wally" Baker left the cinema in 1931 and the management continued, until 1937, under his brother-in-law, Albert "Mac" Parker, who had joined the cinema in 1919 as chief operator after service in France during the First World War. He had entered the industry around 1911 when he became an apprentice operator, at the age of thirteen, in his home town of Swadlincote, near Burton-on-Trent, and had been appointed resident manager of the Palladium in the late 1920s.

The cinema was taken over from Monday 22 May 1933 by a new company, Palladium (Stockport) Ltd.; all the shareholders were local people, and included among them was Harold Brooke. The company was headed by managing director J. T. L. Mallard, who had run a radio shop on Sandy Lane, South Reddish. The cinema underwent redecoration and renovation, and was fitted with new lighting; it became the New Palladium from 14 September that year. In 1937 there was talk of installing a balcony at the cinema, or converting it into a Dance Hall, but neither scheme came to fruition, and in September control passed to Richmond Cinemas, under the management of J. T. L. Mallard's brother, A. J. Mallard.

In May 1939 J. T. L. Mallard returned, having formed Tegarn Cinema Ltd., and again took control of the Palladium; Joseph W. Arnison, a director of the company, and ex-manager of the Wellington, served as manager. The name of the company derived from parts of Arnison's surname, and those of his wife, and fellow director. Florence Arnison's maiden name was Teggin. In 1944 Tegarn also acquired the Wellington.

One employee remembered: "as a full-time cashier my wage was £1 15s. 0d. Many of the usherettes worked all day in the mill, and came straight on to earn their 'holiday money' for the wakes week's holiday. We had a very elderly doorman called Albert, I never knew his second name, but I can remember him clearly standing in the foyer shouting '9d., 1s. 0d. and 1s. 9d.', this was the seat prices. Many times it was standing room only or house full, especially on a Saturday".

The two cinemas were taken over by the Essoldo circuit in 1948. Joseph W. Arnison

The Palladium Cinema in 1955 shortly before it closed.

left to join J. T. L. Mallard in the running of the Siddall Ice Cream Company in Ashton-Under-Lyne. Vincent O'Brien was the cinema's manager from 1948 to May 1953, and the last manager was John A. Metcalfe. In January 1955 the building was purchased by Wilmslow millionaire, and furniture store owner, Harry Brooks. It was first reported that the cinema would close in February, but it was later announced that the lease had a number of years to run. However on 25 February the following year the cinema closed. It was the second cinema in the town operated by the Essoldo group to close that year. The final programme offered Randolph Scott in *Rage at Dawn*, supported by Julie Bishop in *Why Men Leave Home*.

The building was sold to Henry's Stores Ltd., and after a considerable reconstruction opened as a department store the following year. It is still in use as a store, but the side and back walls running down Hatton Street, and Bridgefield Street, remain from its previous life as a cinema.

Don

The Don Picture Palace, on Bramhall Lane, was close to the junction with Wellington Road South; it was opened on 25 September 1913. The original owner was Walter Hapwood, who at one time ran a shop next to the Blossoms Hotel. The site had previously been occupied by several very old cottages. The company known as The Don Picture Palace Co. Ltd. was run by General Manager Daniel Garner, and there was seating for about 700, including a balcony, which could not be used on opening due to a ban by the Watch Committee. In 1919 an application to open it to the public was successful, on condition that nobody was allowed to stand. Early in 1914 the cinema was taken over by Rossendale Cinemas based in Liverpool.

Talking pictures were first shown on Monday 12 May 1930, when *Sunny Side Up*, a Fox musical was shown. Shortly before this the cinema had undergone alterations and thirty nine seats had been added. In October 1933 the company was reorganised as Rossendale Cinemas (1933) Ltd., and in February 1936 ownership passed to a new local company headed by Fred Thorniley, the chairman and managing director. Thorniley was also chairman of the Alexandra Cinema Co. (Edgeley) Ltd.; the two cinemas were run together in 1936-37, and again from 1940, until his retirement in 1949, by General Manager Arthur Hulme Redfern. Redfern had been the cinema's manager between 1922 and 1929, when he left to become manager of the Alexandra. His replacement at the Don had been F. H. Simmonds, who worked at the cinema as an operator for twelve years. He left to take up a position with the company in Ellesmere Port in February 1935, but the following year returned to the town as general manager of the Star and Edgeley cinemas. Reginald W. Trotter, from Liverpool, a director of the company, then became manager, but was replaced by T. V. Stephenson as resident manager when the cinema was taken over. Arthur Redfern died in February 1953, aged sixty one. Felix Dawson became general manager in 1949.

The cinema was closed on 29 June 1957. The final programme featured Norman Wisdom in *Up in the World*. The reasons given were the usual ones of the high rate of Entertainment Tax, and the loss of audiences to television; to which was added the inability to convert the building for the showing of widescreen films. The manageress on closure, Mrs. Bertha Morley, had started at the cinema twenty six years before as an usherette, and her husband, then a projectionist, had started twenty eight years before as a violinist in the cinema orchestra.

The building was sold for a "substantial sum" to John Blundell Ltd., a subsidiary of United Draperies Ltd., and was reopened as a store. It remained in this use until about 1985, reopening in 1986 as a furniture store.

The Don Cinema in 1957 a week before closure.

King's

The King's cinema on Bentley Street, Lancashire Hill, was formally opened on 31 October 1913. It seated 950, with the cheaper seating on forms, and the more expensive on tip-up seats upholstered in leather. The building had a 90′ by 45′ auditorium, described on opening as "lofty and well-ventilated", steam heating throughout and a floor slope of one foot in nine. It was built for Bailey's Estate Co. Ltd., by R. Castle and Son of Reddish, and the first licencee was John Thomas Bailey.

The cinema's early days were troubled ones. The cinematograph licence was issued subject to a direct telephone link to the fire station being fitted, a usual condition of the time, and on 29 November 1913 the cinema was closed when it was discovered that this link had not been fitted. In July 1915 proceedings were taken against John Bailey for failing to apply for a renewal of the cinematograph licence, and the following month the licence was transferred to Leonard George Bailey. Leonard Bailey was born in Manchester in 1890, and educated at Eccles Grammar School. Between 1910 and 1915 he had managed cinemas in Bradford, Manchester and Ashton. In October the following year a police inspection discovered him to be away on military service, and his sister Martha in charge. The cinema was again closed until a "satisfactory" person took charge, and the telephone link was returned to working order. The following month a licence was issued to Martha Bailey.

Walter Charlesworth ran the cinema from 1917 to 1921, when it was again taken over by Leonard Bailey on behalf of the Manchester and District Picture House Company Ltd. The company was formed in August 1920 to acquire five cinemas in the Manchester area; one of its buildings was the Albert Hall. The company was soon in financial difficulties, and on 1 May 1924 renewal of the cinematograph licence was deferred due to non payment of rates. A week later it was renewed for only three months following payment of the previous year's rates, and an agreement to pay the current year's rates by instalment. However, in January 1925 the cinema was taken over by a receiver appointed by the company's debenture holders, and the following year the company was wound up. Leonard Bailey later formed a small cinema circuit in the Manchester area.

In September 1925 Ernest Wardle from Bolton took over as proprietor, and moved to Heaton Chapel. Wardle had been a town councillor in Bolton during the 1920s, and had also managed the Gem cinema there for many years. On leaving the King's he returned to Bolton, where he died in April 1943, aged eighty. The King's was one of the last of the town's cinemas to install sound equipment. The first talking picture shown, *The Love Parade*, opened on 6 April 1931. One benefit from this delay lay in the technical improvement made in sound systems since the early days of talkies; this gave cinemas who installed them later a better sound reproduction. Two long serving employees, well remembered by the cinema's patrons, were Annie Miller, who worked in the paybox, and Stanley Johnson, known as "Johnty", who sold ice cream and chocolates.

In November 1939 George S. Smith took over, and continued to run the cinema until it closed in late 1960. Smith, who lived on Gorton Road, Reddish, later ran a number of other cinemas in the Manchester area, including, from November 1946, the Grove, and from 1956 the Olympia on Hyde Road. He was also a shareholder in the Savoy Cinema, Romiley, during the 1950s, and he moved to Prestwich after taking over the Plaza Cinema there. During the war when the cinema's operator was called into the forces, usherette Emily Hulme trained for the job, becoming one of the two women operators in the town (the other at the Carlton). After the war Emily Hulme became manager of the Grove, and later the Olympia, before returning to the King's as its final manager in 1959. At the time estate agents were seeking permission from the town's planning committee for a change of use for the building. George Smith, beset by financial problems, died suddenly at his home in March, 1961, aged fifty nine. After closure the building was used for Bingo, and it opened in June 1963 as the King's Casino, before disappearing in the redevelopment of the area in the mid 1960s.

The King's Cinema, Bentley Street, 1961. The slope of the ground made it an ideal site for a cinema auditorium. However, it was the archetypal "flea pit!"

Brinksway Pictorium

The first performance at the Brinksway Pictorium was on Thursday, 6 November 1913, and music was provided by Miss Lucy Fenney at the piano. Prices were 2d, 4d., 6d. and 9d., with the cheapest seats at 3d. on Saturdays and holidays. The cinema, designed by local architects J. E. Wrathnell and Warren Blackshaw, had a frontage—it remained intact until it was demolished—faced with Buxton brick, and an auditorium seating 420. The original proprietor was Isaac Redfern, who died in January 1919; afterwards his wife Sarah took over as manager. Two years later Redfern's son, Arthur, took charge, having been associated with the cinema since it opened. He was later to manage the Don and Alexandra cinemas.

A pianist of the early 1920s remembers that: "the piano was concealed behind a curtain at the foot of the screen, but when seated at the piano the top of one's head protruded above the curtain rail. The light for the music stand was a low power bulb with a metal shade. This also served to illuminate the target for the orange peel, apple core and pea-shooter marksmen, who were notably accurate".

In March 1923 the licence passed briefly to William Wright, before Harry Butterworth took over in August; he ran the cinema until 1927. In April that year Harry Frearson took over as manager for proprietor, John Mills, of Edgeley. Following John Mills' death in 1931, Frearson and Mrs. Martha Mills formed a new company in 1932 to run the cinema. Frearson acted as managing director until the following year, when he left to open a jewellery business in School Lane, Heaton Chapel. The cinema was one of the last in the town to fit sound equipment, continuing to show silent films into

The Brinksway Pictorium in 1973.

March 1931. In July 1933 Mrs. Jennie Hulme took over the licence, remaining until the cinema was closed in October the following year.

The new proprietor was Gordon Ray, ex-principal comedian with the Vaudevillians; he installed new sound equipment, and effected a number of other alterations, before reopening the cinema on 7 January 1935. His policy was to mix variety acts—including himself—and films, in what he called "cine-variety". A few weeks later the cinema began to be advertised as the New Pictorium. Prices were 5d, 7d. and 9d., and the cinema was open from 6.30 p.m. to 10.30 p.m. The Saturday matinees—"Uncle Gordon always looks after his little pals"—are remembered for Gordon Ray's contribution of sand dances wearing a fez, and other routines. After fifty years Ray is still remembered for his generosity during those depression years; he often admitted poorer children free to the Saturday matinee. He attempted to revive the Queen's cinema with a similar policy in the same year, but does not appear to have succeeded with either cinema.

In July 1937 the cinema was taken over by James Caton, who was to retain control until it closed in 1958. Caton lived on Marple Road, Offerton, and was born in Manchester, but emigrated to Canada in 1902. He worked on the construction of the Canadian Pacific Railway, and also travelled in New Zealand, Australia and North and South America, before returning to England in 1920. In 1929 he formed Suburban Cinemas (Manchester), which ran a number of cinemas in the North West. James Caton died, aged seventy nine, in March 1961.

On 10 May 1958 the cinema closed for redecoration and re-seating, and was advertised to reopen in August. Though the plan was approved by the Watch Committee in July, it appears never to have reopened. The cinema was by this time changing its programme four times a week, and its final programme, for Friday and Saturday, was *Gunfight at the O.K. Corral* in Vistavision and Technicolour. Its admission prices were 1s. 0d. and 1s. 6d. After closure as a cinema the building was used as a warehouse for a number of years until about 1976, after which it stood empty. In January 1978 a fire gutted the building and shortly afterwards it was demolished.

Final programme poster of the Brinksway Pictorium 1958. In spite of the note at the bottom of the poster it never re-opened.

The Alexandra Cinema, Castle Street, Edgeley, 1961, about the time of closure.

Alexandra

The Alexandra, on Castle Street, was one of the town's largest pre-First World War cinemas. It was erected in about twelve weeks by W. B. Beattie and Co., of King Street West, for the Alexandra Cinema Co. (Edgeley) Ltd. The front of the building was originally picked out in the old English style of black and white, and there was a spacious tiled entrance hall. The auditorium, measuring 80′ by 45′, seated about 900.

The cinema opened on Monday 22 December 1913. The first programme included: "*The Call*—a fine Vitagraph drama and a screaming Keystone comedy—*A Chip off the Old Block*". Prices were 6d. and 3d. The cinema was closed on 12 May 1928. The company had acquired three shops on the Greek Street side of the cinema, and this site was used to extend the auditorium and entrance. A balcony was also added, increasing the seating to 1300. The Alexandra reopened as virtually a new cinema on 19 September 1928, showing *Seventh Heaven* starring Janet Gaynor and Charles Farrell. It was now the town's leading cinema, a position it consolidated in the following year when it became the first in the town to install sound equipment.

Al Jolson as *The Singing Fool* opened on Saturday, 3 August 1929, and proved so successful that it was retained for a further two weeks. The second talkie programme *Showboat* was also held over for a further week. The Alexandra again asserted its place as one of the town's leading cinemas when it became the first to provide a car park. The management announced in March 1932: "that they now possess a first class enclosed car park for one hundred cars".

Arthur H. Redfern was appointed manager in 1929, and served as general manager from 1931 to 1937. In September of that year the cinema was taken over by David Forrester Theatres Ltd. (also known as Jefton Entertainments Ltd.); it was run first from London, and later from a Manchester office. The company ran about seven other cinemas, but was soon in financial difficulties and was wound up in 1940. In June 1940 the cinema was closed for redecoration and renovation, and reopened on 5 August 1940 with George Formby in *Come on George*. The building was under the renewed proprietorship

The Alexandra Cinema from an architect's drawing of 1928.

of the Alexandra Cinema Co. (Edgeley) Ltd., and the "personal supervision" of Arthur H. Redfern, now also General Manager of the Don. Chairman of the company, Fred Thorniley, a well-known local businessman, and a past president of the local Cinematograph Exhibitors Associaition, died suddenly in October 1943, aged sixty eight. His two sons, Fred and Eric were also directors of the company.

A fire was discovered in the balcony during the early hours of Tuesday 15 July 1952; it destroyed fifty seats, and part of the balcony floor. The cinema was shut for over three months, during which time it was rewired, refitted and decorated. It reopened on Monday 3 November showing Burt Lancaster in *Ten Tall Men*.

The Alexandra survived into the 1960s under manager Joseph M. Brooks, who joined the cinema from the Essoldo group during the 1950s. On 4 November 1961 the cinema was closed; the final programme offered a double bill of X certificate films, *Portrait of a Mobster* and *Girl of the Night*. Eric Thorniley announced that the cinema had been sold to a property development company, and their intentions were not known. The building was later converted to use as a supermarket.

Vernon

A cinematograph licence was issued to Ernest Hadfield in respect of the Vernon Picture Palace, Carrington Road, on 22 December 1913. The cinema, which seated about 500, was originally run by the Vernon Picture Palace company, with Hadfield as licencee, until 1915; in that year B. Mainwaring Dunston took over as proprietor. Thomas Knott and his brother then managed the cinema from 1921 to 1930. Knott, who later became manager of the Grove Cinema in Hazel Grove, had worked at his father's mill engineer's works in the Lower Carrs, before service in the First World War. Invalided home, he worked at a mill in Portwood, and for a haulage firm run by his brother, until taking over the Vernon. He died in January 1955, aged seventy nine. Two pianists who played at the cinema during the 1920s were Phyllis Stubbs, the daughter of a herbalist in Portwood, and Mabel Perry, cousin of Fred Perry, the tennis player. For four hours solo playing each evening they were paid 2s. 6d.

In December 1930 the cinema was still defiantly advertising itself as the "Vernon (Silent) Cinema", with admission prices of 8d., 5d. and 4d.; this was well below the prices charged by cinemas showing talkies. Sound equipment was installed the following year, and an additional row of seats was also fitted. Harold Lowe took over as proprietor in 1930, and remained until the cinema was closed in September 1936. It was reopened on 21 December that year by Northern Amusements Ltd., of Rochdale, who ran it until closure. The cinema had been redecorated, and reseated, and new carpets and curtains fitted. The company was managed by secretary and director Eugene Hamson, who also ran the Savoy in Heaton Moor. The reopening programme offered Shirley Temple in *The Littlest Rebel*, with seat prices of 6d. and 9d., and 3d. and 5d. for children. Harry Smith, the manager, was to remain with the cinema until a few months before it was closed; at that point a Mr. Hamson took over as manager.

The Vernon Cinema, Carrington Road, Portwood, in 1961, shortly before demolition.

An outline proposal to redevelop the site as a service station was passed by the town's planning committee in August 1957, and in October a letter of protest was sent to the town council by the local Conservative party regarding the imminent closure of the cinema. The Vernon was closed on 6 December 1958; the final programme was a Walt Disney double bill, *Davy Crockett* and *The African Lion*.

Wellington

Plans were first submitted for a cinema on the site of the Borough Carriage Company's old premises, close to the junction of Higher Hillgate and Wellington Road South, in 1916, but the Wellington Picture House was not opened until Monday, 11 July 1921. The opening was performed by James Fernley J.P., chairman of the Watch Committee, and Mr. H. Cross, managing director of the Wellington (Stockport) Picture House Co. Ltd. The cinema seated just over 1000. The building also included a billiard hall, with thirteen tables and an "up-to-date cafe". The manager was F. W. Walters, and the first week offered, amongst other delights, *Only a Mill Girl* with "Hay Foxwell in his original role". Performances were continuous from 3.00 p.m. to 10.30 p.m. and admission prices were 1s. 6d., 9d., and 7d., with 9d., 6d. and 4d. charged before 5.00 p.m.

Early programmes included Mary Pickford in *Pollyanna* (August), and Douglas Fairbanks in *The Mark of Zorro* (October). Early 1922 saw the additional attraction of song pictures. Vocalists Arnold Bennett, Louise Platt and Fred Hill, with the Theatre orchestra, accompanied films, and illustrated songs such as Sally in our Alley, and Home Sweet Home. Frank H. Hough became general manager in 1922, and February 1929 saw the cinema showing Cecil B. De Mille's silent epic *King of Kings*. The film had been refused a certificate by the British Board of Film Censors, who objected to the portrayal of Christ in person, but the Watch Committee passed it for local screening.

Talking pictures opened on 17 February 1930, offering Billie Dove in *Her Private Life;* this was supported by Walter Pidgeon in *Love is Like a Rose*, and a Mickey Mouse cartoon. The following week's programme was Alfred Hitchcock's *Blackmail*, the first British talkie. Charles J. Spittle became manager in late 1933, and the cinema's advertisements became his "weekly chat", describing the cinema as the "cosy family cinema". Prices were now 1s 0d., 9d. and 6d. Spittle was soon followed, from May 1934, by Joseph W. Arnison who remained until 1939. Harry Hampson was then appointed manager; he become well-known for his Tuesday night "Discoveries," a local talent show he organised, and Friday night "Merrymakers."

The Wellington Cinema, at the junction of Higher Hillgate and Wellington Road, during its final week as a cinema in August 1963.

In October 1944 the company, by now associated with the Charles Ogden circuit based in Manchester, went into receivership, and the cinema was taken over by Tegarn Cinemas Ltd. The licence was held by the cinema's ex-manager, now a director of the Tegarn company, Joseph W. Arnison, who already managed the Palladium. The new management redecorated, and partially reseated the cinema, and effected a number of other improvements which resulted in improved attendances. In 1948 Tegarn was taken over by the Essoldo group, who continued to run the cinema until 1963.

In the late 1950s the cinema often showed the same programme as the Astor; the exotic fare included *6-5 Special*, the nudist film *Isle of Levant*, and *Grip of the Strangler* with Boris Karloff. In contrast it also advertised its "big children's matinee, including free comics and sweets, at prices of 6d. and 9d." The cafe, which became known as the Manor Lounge, was for a time during the pop boom of the early 1960s, a club presenting local groups.

In 1961 the cinema began to be used for bingo on one night a week, but rumours of closure were denied. The cinema was closed on 31 August 1963; its last offering was a Hayley Mills week, and the final film was *Pollyanna*. The building was leased to Coulson Enterprises, of Wakefield, as a bingo hall, and was later run by the Essoldo circuit and the Ladbroke group. In 1986 it was renamed Walker's Social Club.

Savoy

When notices appeared in June 1921 on Heaton Moor Road, identifying the proposed site of a cinema, there was an immediate outcry from local residents, especially church groups. In August a petition was presented to the town council by resident groups opposed to the proposal, and the subject was further debated in the town council in October. Despite the objections digging operations were reported to have started in June 1922.

The opening of the Savoy cinema took place on Monday, 19 March 1923, and was performed by the Mayor, Alderman Charles Royle. The opening film presented Lady Diana Manners in *The Virgin Queen*, with orchestral music supplied by Constance Cross's Ladies Orchestra. The following day an injunction was granted in the County Court to prevent the cinema from continuing to show this film. Stockport Palace Ltd., proprietors of the Prince's and Super cinemas, had agreed a fee of £50 (for a six-day run) with the film's distributor, The Rose Film Co. Ltd., for the first showing of the film in the town. As this was not to have been until the following month, legal action was taken to prevent the showing at the Savoy.

The cinema designed by architects Pierce and Son, with seating for 1013, was built by contractors R. Bardsley and Son for James Francis Kelly, and town councillor James Harrison. They continued to run it until 1930. The cinema was then taken over by the Hippodrome (Accrington) Ltd., who fitted sound equipment. In October 1932 R. C. Roy, a Didsbury builder, and proprietor of the Capitol cinema, formed Lancashire County Theatres Ltd.; he took over the Hippodrome, Accrington, and four other cinemas in the Manchester area, including the Savoy. Roy would later build one of Manchester's largest cinemas, the Apollo, Ardwick, and served on the board of directors of the company which owned it.

The Savoy Cinema, Heaton Moor Road, c. 1931.

The Savoy Cinema, Heaton Moor Road, 1986.

In July 1934 Northern Amusements Ltd., incorporated in April, took control. Eugene Hamson, secretary and a director of the company, lived on Heaton Moor Road and continued to hold the licence until 1948. In April and May 1936 the cinema was completely redecorated, reseated with "super luxury seats", and new lighting and projection equipment fitted. During the 1930s the seating was reduced to just over 800.

In 1938 disaster was narrowly adverted when fire swept through the building. The fire was discovered on Tuesday night, 15 March, by the manager, A. Birchenough, only minutes after the audience of 600, for Flora Robson and Leslie Banks in *Farewell Again*, had left the building. The cinema was closed, reopening on Monday 4 July, the same day as the Super cinema which had also been closed in March by a fire. The roof had been totally replaced, but the cinema remained identical to that destroyed by the fire. The reopening programme offered Paul Muni in *The Life of Emile Zola*.

In 1948 the cinema was taken over by Tatton Cinemas (Gatley) Ltd. Formed in February 1937 by Nash Eaton, with a capital of £12,000, the company had opened its first cinema, the Tatton, in Gatley, in October of that year. That cinema's manageress, and later proprietor after the death of Nash Eaton in 1957, was Vera Edge. Her son, Jack, began: ". . . his career as a white-gloved, pillbox hatted pageboy, opening car doors for patrons at the Tatton cinema". He took over as manager of the Savoy from July 1948, and is now Chairman and Managing Director of the company based at the Davenport Theatre. The Savoy initially opened on Sundays after this was allowed in 1946, but was soon returned to six day opening by the new proprietors, a policy which continues today.

The taste of local audiences can perhaps be gauged by the reaction to two films shown in the late 1950s. In 1958 the Hammer Films version of *Dracula* was taken off after three days, following protests and poor box office takings, but the following year *Carry on Nurse* did such good business that it was held over for a second week.

The cinema was closed on 5 December 1970 for modernisation. "We start shaping the ultimate in luxury cinemagoing", proclaimed the advertisements. When it was reopened, in the presence of the Mayor, on Wednesday, 19 May 1971, as the New Savoy, the balcony had been removed, the seating reduced and the foyer extended at the front of the building. The reopening presentation was *There's a Girl in My Soup* with Peter Sellers and Goldie Hawn.

Controversy returned in 1982 when protesters picketed the cinema during the showing of *Who Dares Wins*. The cinema was again closed by fire in October 1986. Vandals had hid in the cinema after closing, set alight the stage curtains and the fire destroyed the screen. The cinema was closed for six days, but reopened after the installation of a new screen.

The interior of the Savoy Cinema, Heaton Moor Road, in 1936 and 1986 respectively.

Hippodrome

Astor

The first of the national circuits to appear in the town was Associated British Cinemas, who took over the Hippodrome Theatre in 1932. The Hippodrome was located at the market end of St. Petersgate, with a side entrance on High Street. It was opened on 4 September 1905 as the Empire Theatre; it was built on the site of the Grand Theatre, which had been pulled down in 1904. Films were shown as early as 1896 at the Grand, and the Empire's first programme included Vernon's Imperial Bioscope: thereafter it regularly included films as part of its bill. In January 1910 the theatre received one of the first two cinematograph licences issued in the town, but film shows were later limited to fifteen minutes duration. Its name was changed to the Hippodrome in February 1915.

From early 1921 to mid 1922 the licence was held by J. H. Stansfield, managing director of Stockport Palace Ltd., and proprietor of the Prince's and Super cinemas. The historical epic *The Power of the Borgias* was shown in seven parts on Good Friday 1921, but the theatre remained largely dedicated to live performances.

Entrance to Astor Cinema, St. Petersgate, in March 1952.

In July 1931 the theatre was taken over by Harry Buxton, who ran a number of cinemas throughout the country. Buxton had in his youth worked as a call boy at the Hippodrome, and hit the headlines in 1928 when he won £65,000 at the casino in Nice. Western Electric sound equipment was installed, and the theatre reopened as a cinema on 3 August 1931. The opening ceremony was performed by Belle Chrystal: "A British International Film Star, who has just completed *Hindle Wakes*". The first week's programme offered the film *Her Unborn Child*, and a personal appearance of Horatio Bottomley: "The ex-MP (the man who should have been Prime Minister of England), just returned from abroad, and will address the audience at each performance". The cinema seated 899, and prices were 6d. and 1s. 0d., with 6d., 9d. and 1s. 3d. being charged on Saturdays and holidays. The licencee and manager was John Pickles. One of the early attractions was a *Stockport Film Review* which invited the audience to: "see yourself on the screen". Some of the big films of the year included: *Hell's Angels* in September, *Dracula* in October, Charlie Chaplin's *City Lights* (retained for three weeks) in November, and *Little Caesar*, the film which made a star of Edward G. Robinson, in December. There was also a visit to the cinema by another forgotten British film star, Dodo Watts, in September.

In January 1932 the cinema was taken over by the A.B.C. circuit. When A.B.C. absorbed the Union Cinemas circuit it gained control of the town's largest cinema, the Ritz, and vacated the Hippodrome on 8 January 1938. Control passed to Richmond Cinemas, a company based in Liverpool, which ran a number of cinemas in Lancashire; these included the Palladium in Stockport. In 1940 variety acts became regular Friday night features until the cinema was closed on 2 March 1940. The last film featured Bob Burns in *Our Leading Citizen*. The theatre was closed for three weeks for renovation, and reopened as a variety theatre. From 1943 it became the home of Frank H. Fortescue's repertory company.

On 3 December 1951 the theatre, renamed the Astor, was reopened as a cinema by Woodhill Entertainments; the managing director of the company was Sydney

The Astor Cinema, St. Petersgate, in 1965. "A Bucket of Blood", was never shown because the cinema was damaged by fire.

Shurman. The opening presented a personal appearance of Randolph Turpin, ex-middleweight champion of the World; the main film attraction which followed was a boxing picture starring Jeff Chandler, and called *The Iron Man*. By this time prices were 10d. and 1s. 0d. for stalls, 1s. 6d. for the circle, and 2s. 1d. for the dress circle; and the seating capacity was also increased to 960. The nature of future programmes was signposted by the second week's attraction, the X certificate French film *Clochemerle*. Mixed with the normal commercial fare, a number of other foreign films were shown in the early 1950s; they included Max Ophulus' *Le Plaisir*, and Akira Kurosawa's *Rashomon*.

In September 1955 Tatler Entertainments, better known as the Orr Circuit of Coventry, took over. The following May a lorry damaged the pillars supporting the canopy at the front of the building, and it had to be removed. At this time the manager was John Metcalfe, who had been manager at the Palladium when it closed. He was replaced by Mrs. Lilian May, whom he had replaced; she was to finally leave the cinema in November 1959 to run a pub in Hyde. Her replacement was Harry Smith, who had managed the Vernon cinema for twenty five years until shortly before its closure in 1958. Previously Smith had managed the Princess cinema in Dukinfield.

During the late 1950s programmes became largely horror and other X certificate films; this is evident from the programme of Thursday, 27 November 1958, when the cinema was closed by the police because of an unsafe roof. The films showing were *It, the Terror from Beyond Space*, and *The Curse of the Faceless Man*. The cinema reopened, after repairs, in January 1959, with the film *Juvenile Passion*. The local press also pointed to the programming policy, with a story headed, "Nudes in High Street", during the cinema's run of the nudist film *Isle of Levant* in 1958. In contrast, a special Saturday matinee for children was run as The Roy Rogers Club.

The cinema was closed after being badly damaged by a fire; this was discovered at about 11.20 p.m. on Saturday, 5 March 1960. Although various plans were put forward the cinema never reopened. The final programme had offered a triple bill: the French film *A Woman of Evil, The Mask* and the Goons short *The Case of the Mukkinese Battlehorn*. The cinema had continued to programme just enough interesting films to ensure that the Astor was sorely missed by the town's discerning filmgoers.

The poster for the following week's programme—which never opened—*A Bucket of Blood*, and *The Headless Ghost*, continued to amuse passers by for a number of years. The theatre itself was demolished in 1965, but the frontage remained standing until 1968. The site is now occupied by a block of offices.

Plaza

The Plaza Cinema, Mersey Square, under construction in 1932.

The plans drawn up by architect W. Thorniley for the Plaza super cinema, were first submitted to the town council for approval in April 1929; the company, the Plaza Cinema (Stockport) Ltd., was registered in December 1930, and had a capital of £50,000. The chairman of the company was Fred Read, with Alfred Snape and Arthur L. Ward serving as joint managing directors. Together they controlled a number of cinemas in the Manchester area, and were known as the Read, Snape and Ward circuit. The Plaza was built on the site of old cottages facing Mersey Square; construction proved extremely difficult because of the need to cut the foundations out of solid rock.

A private show was given on Friday, 7 October 1932, when the Mayor, Councillor James Penny, J.P., performed the opening ceremony. The first public show, held the following evening, was a charity performance for Stockport Infirmary. The films shown were *Out of the Blue*, starring Gene Gerrard and Jessie Matthews, and Laurel and Hardy in *Jailbirds*. Regular shows, continuous except for Saturday, started the following Monday, with Fredric March in *Dr. Jekyll and Mr. Hyde*. The first manager, George L. Abercrombie, joined the cinema from the Kingsway in Levenshulme. Prices ranged from 7d. for the stalls to 2s 0d. for the Royal Circle in the evening, and from 5d. to 1s. 0d. before 4 p.m. The cinema also offered sunray treatment to waiting patrons from the "Neron Vitalux Lamp" located in the foyer. Seating was provided for 700 in the balcony, and 1170 in

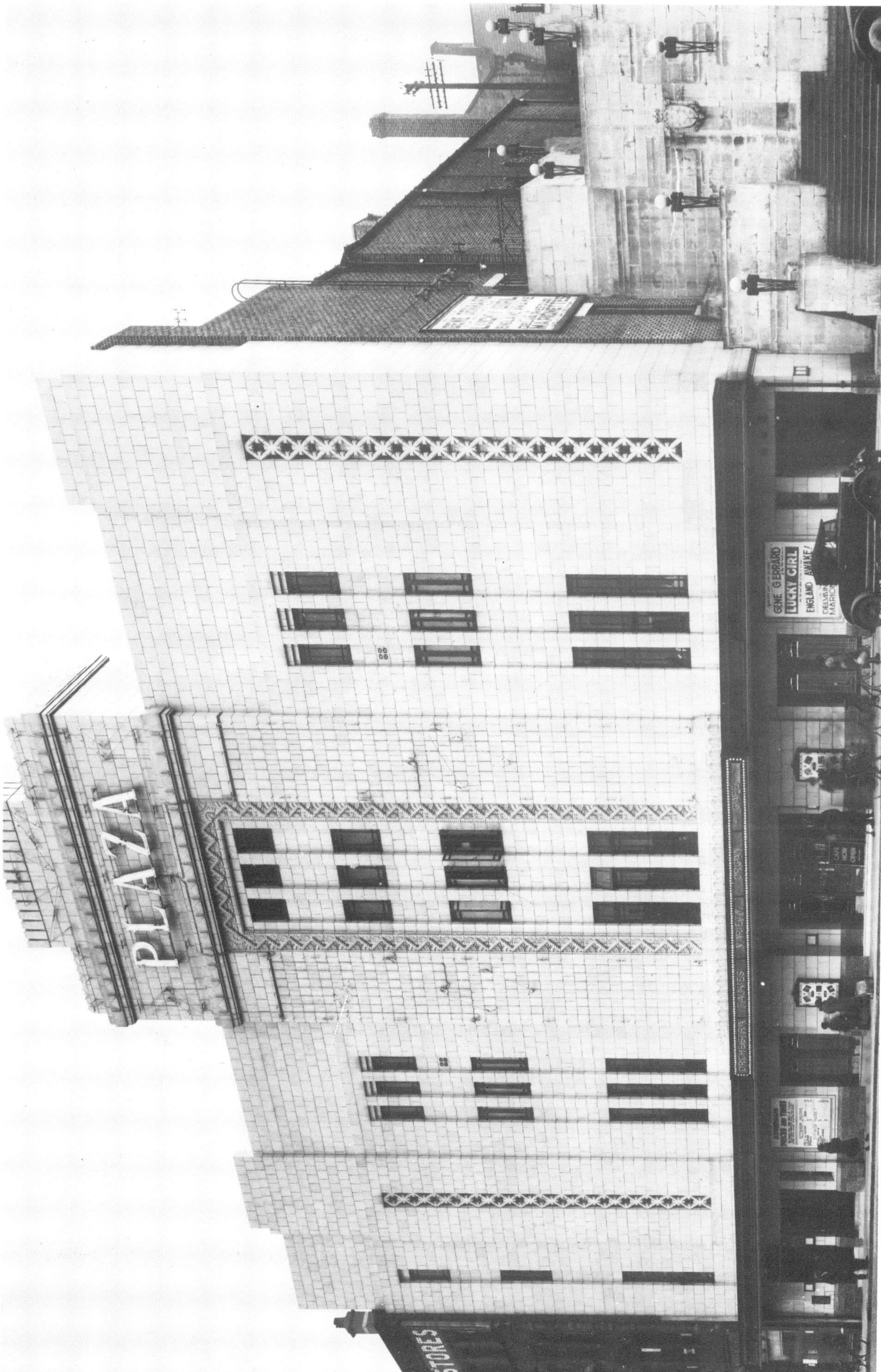

The Plaza Cinema, Mersey Square, shortly after opening in 1932.

the stalls. The building also contained a cafe, situated behind the balcony, which looked out over Mersey Square.

Early programmes included live acts, but by the end of 1934 these had mostly disappeared. The Compton organ, however, was to prove a more lasting feature. The first organist, Cecil Chadwick, stayed eight months, to be replaced by Harry D. Speed who left in March 1940 to join the ABC circuit. Speed later went into cinema management, and was manager of the Rota when it closed in 1959. The organ remained in use until the early 1960s, with William Starr appearing every Saturday night.

In October 1934 George Abercrombie was appointed manager of the Broadway Theatre, Eccles, and was succeeded at the Plaza by Oliver Howlinson. Fred Read died in September 1933, and the group now became known as the Snape and Ward circuit. W. F. Maxfield, the new manager, took over the licence on the death of Arthur Ward in February 1936. In July of the following year the cinema was closed for three days when fire seriously damaged the stage. The Plaza's longest serving manager was appointed in 1939. Walter Haydn Ellwood remained at the cinema for 13 years, leaving in 1952 to manage the Deansgate cinema in Manchester.

The management of the Plaza Cinema in 1932.

Councillor FRED READ
(*Chairman*)

ALFRED SNAPE
(*Joint Managing Director*)

A. L. WARD
(*Joint Managing Director*)

In January 1958 he left that cinema for home and disappeared. He was later found drowned, and an inquest recorded an open verdict after hearing that he had recently been worried.

After Alfred Snape's death in 1947 the running of the circuit passed to Brian Snape and Harold Ward. The cinema became the first in the town to run the same programme for seven days, when Danny Kaye in *The Secret Life of Walter Mitty*, opened on Sunday 2 October 1949. This did not become general practice in the town's other cinemas for many years. The early 1950s saw visits to the cinema by a number of stars. Jimmy Jewel and Ben Warriss appeared in April 1950 to promote their film *What a Carry On*, David Farrar followed in November 1951 for *The Golden Horde*, and Jack Warner during the screening of *Scrooge* in February 1952.

With the departure of Haydn Ellwood, R. F. Capon became manager in 1952; he was replaced in 1954 by Ian M. Ogilvie. A new screen was fitted in August 1953 in preparation for the showing of Cinemascope films; it cost £1000 and measured 48′ by 18′. The old screen it replaced measured 21′ by 15′. Cinemascope films were not shown until the following year, but the town's first 3-D film, *Sagaree* was shown at the cinema for two weeks in September 1953. It was followed by *Man in the Dark* in November, and *The Maze* and *Fort Ti* in January 1954. In the mid 1950s the Snape and Ward circuit split up, and the Plaza became part of the G. B. Snape circuit. A number of popular Sunday afternoon jazz concerts were held in 1956, including appearances by Ronnie Aldrich and Johnny Dankworth. Some of the big films of the late 1950s first appeared at the Plaza. Cecil B. DeMille's epic, *The Ten Commandments*, opened for a four week run on 31 August 1958, with special prices ranging from 3s. 6d. for front stalls to 7s. 6d. for the circle. *The Bridge on the River Kwai* played for three weeks in April 1958, and *South Pacific* for two weeks in November 1960. A Christmas pantomime, *Babes in the Wood* starring the Dallas Boys, was put on the same year, but did not prove a success, and the idea was not repeated.

In January 1961 Ian Ogilvie commented that contrary to the national decline in cinema admissions, the Plaza's had actually increased annually over the past seven years, with the exception of 1959 which had an exceptionally fine summer. This happy circumstance was not to last. As fewer films were made the more commercial ones were tied up by the big national circuits, represented in the town by the ABC (the Ritz) and Essoldo, and the smaller circuits and independent cinemas were left to play the less attractive films. In July 1965 the cinema was purchased, for a reported £140,000, by the Mecca Group, whose request for a change of use to Bingo was turned down by the Town Council. The battle continued until the end of the following year; permission was finally granted for Bingo on a trial period of two years, after an appeal by Mecca to the Minister of Housing and Local Government resulted in him overruling the local authority's decision. The cinema was closed on 31 December 1966. Its final programme was Jerry Lewis in *Three on a Couch*, and Audie Murphy in *The Texican*. The Plaza reopened as a Bingo hall on 6 February 1967, and remains in this use today.

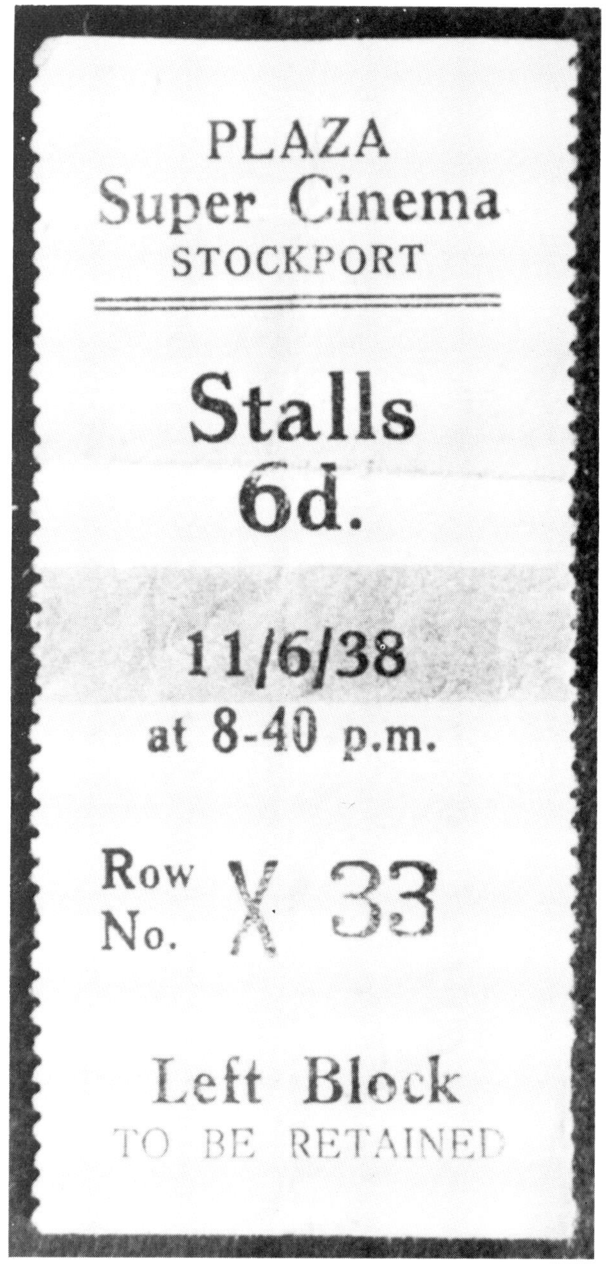

Plaza Cinema ticket in 1938. The film shown was Deanna Durbin in "100 Men and a Girl".

Curzon

The year 1937 was to prove a good year for the town's cinemagoers. Three new cinemas opened in June and, in October, the Marcliff in Hazel Grove, and the Tatton in Gatley, made their debut. The Ritz was also under construction, and due for opening in January 1938.

The first to open its doors, on Saturday, 12 June 1937, was the Curzon on Turncroft Lane; this was operated throughout its life as a cinema by Offerton Cinemas Ltd. Although registered as a separate company the Curzon was part of a small circuit which also included the New Curzon, Flixton, and the Savoy, Romiley. It was a common business practice of the day to register each cinema in a circuit as a separate company, so that if one ran into financial difficulties the circuit could continue. During the 1930s over 2,000 new houses had been built in the area surrounding the cinema, thus providing a ready-made local audience.

The formal opening was performed by Alderman John Coupe, and Frederick S. Eaton; the latter was managing director of Offerton Cinemas Ltd. In the afternoon almost 800 children were admitted free, and in the evening the first regular audience paid 1s. 3d., 1s. 0d., 9d. and 6d. to see Claude Hulbert and Gordon Harker in *Wolf's Clothing*. From the following Monday two performances were offered nightly, and matinees held three times a week (prices 3d. and 6d.), with a special children's matinee on Saturday for 2d. and 3d. Programmes were changed twice weekly, on Monday and Thursday. An important feature, and sign of the changing times, was the provision of a free car park for patrons. During the 1930s most larger cinemas added car

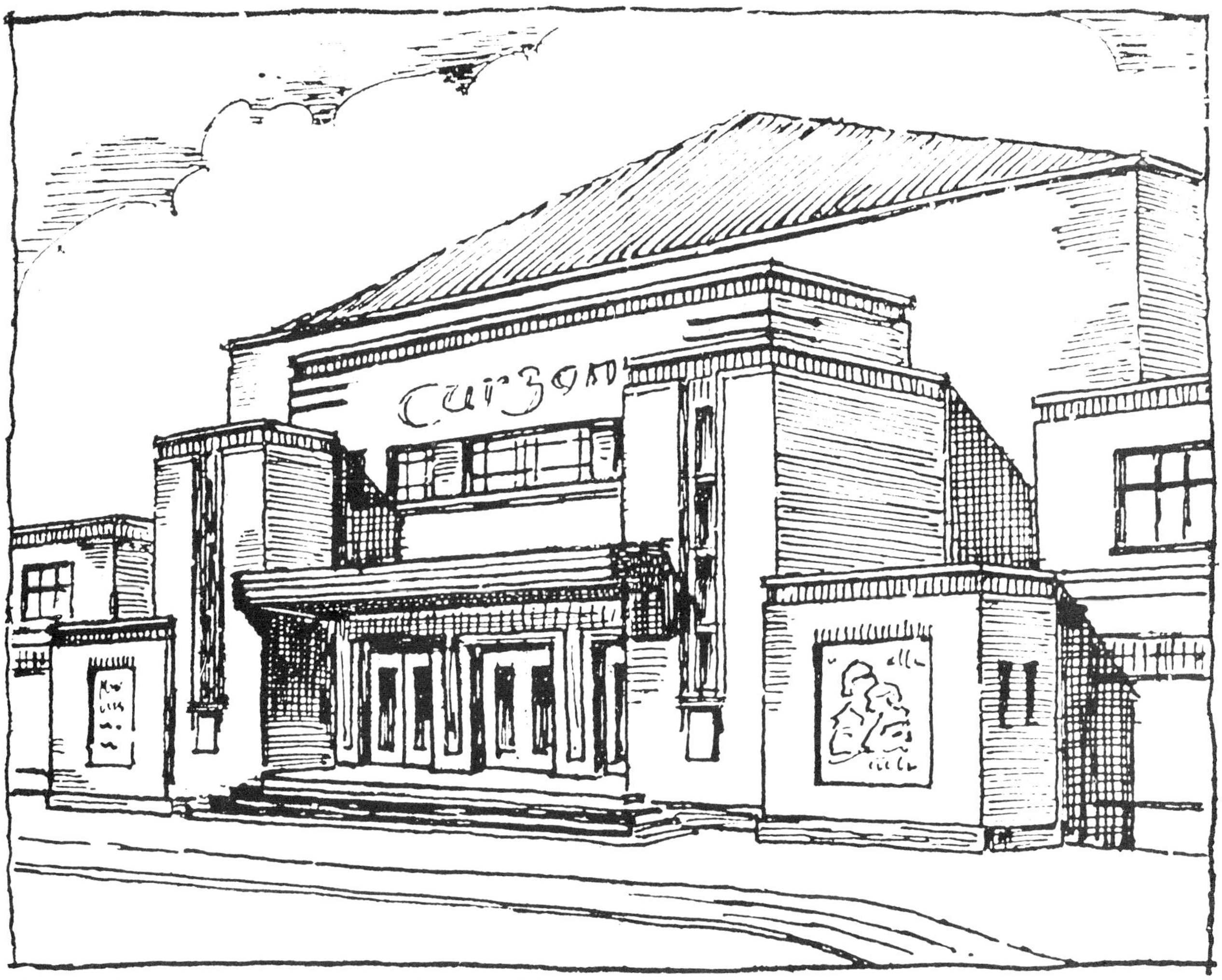

Drawing of the Curzon Cinema, Turncroft Lane, 1937.

The Curzon Cinema, Turncroft Lane, in 1959.

parks, following the Alexandra's lead in 1932, and from now on all the town's new cinemas included one. The building also included two shops on each side of the cinema.

By October the cinema was advertising 400 seats at 6d., 250 at 9d. and 140 at 1s. 0d. The town's industry was represented in March 1938, when local councillor, W. Stanton, introduced The Cotton Queen of Great Britain (and Miss Stockport) before performances of the film *Cotton Queen.* It starred Stanley Holloway and Will Fiffe, and was partially made in Manchester and Blackpool. The Cotton Queen appeared at a number of cinemas in the area to promote the film, and the following month the Stockport heats of the 1938 contest for the title were held at the Carlton cinema. In May 1941 licencee J. A. Woolley was called up into the services, and the licence passed to the cinema's new manager Thomas H. Claughton.

In the late 1940s and early 1950s patrons were treated to serials as a supporting programme, and thrilled to the cliff hanging exploits of Superman and Captain Marvel. The cinema continued to serve its regular local audience into the late 1950s, but was hit by the general fall in admissions. Programmes were now changed three times a week, on Sunday, Tuesday and Thursday. Cinemascope equipment was fitted, but by September 1959 rumours of closure were circulating. The end came on 19 March 1960, with a final programme of *A Private's Affair*, a cinemascope film starring Sal Mineo. J. A. Woolley, director of Offerton Cinemas, and the Curzon's first manager in 1937, blamed television for the closure. The building was converted into a club, reopening in April the following year as the Palace Theatre Club. It remained as a club until the 1970s, and later became Rotters Discotheque. In September 1985 it reopened as Hamilton's, a piano bar and winery.

Davenport

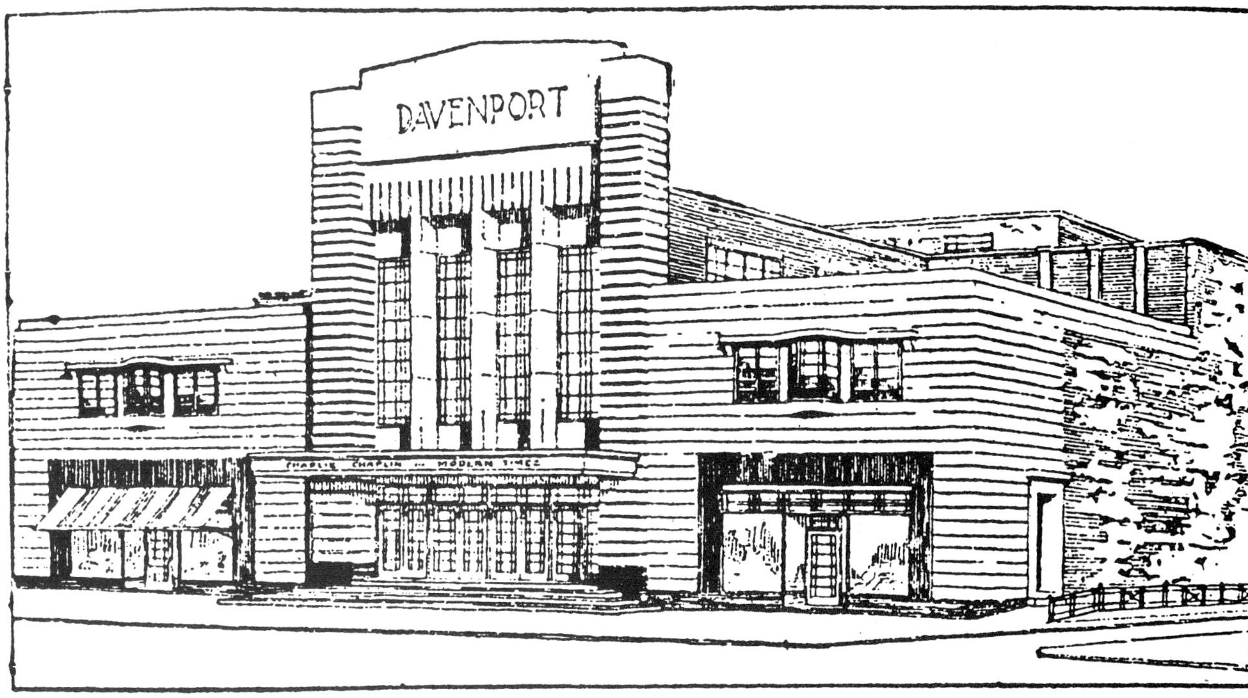

Drawing of the Davenport Cinema, Buxton Road, in 1937.

The opening of the Davenport cinema, Buxton Road, on Thursday 17 June 1937 was performed by the Mayor, Alderman G. Padmore, J.P. The building was designed by a former mayor of Stockport, Charles Hartley, and built on the site of Virginia Cottage, for many years home of Giles Atherton, J.P., Chairman of Stockport Ring Mills Ltd., and three times mayor of the town. Newspaper reports spoke in glowing terms of this new super cinema providing seating for 1750: "On entering the cinema the visitor finds himself in a spacious vestibule, whence two pairs of double doors lead to the auditorium. Over the doors are two mural paintings—the one representing talking pictures, the other the application of electricity to the cinema. In the centre of the vestibule there is an island booking office. Behind it the twin arms of the staircase sweep upwards, and in the recess where the staircase divides, a fountain plays, floodlit in colours and making a very charming sight . . . Art and ingenuity have combined to lead the eye towards the screen . . . Silver flutings sweep across the ceiling and converge towards the orchestra pit".

The opening night programme included Mr. Harold Bettes, the Bournemouth organist, at the Compton organ, and a stage presentation by Millie Jackson's Streamline Six team of dancers. There was a colour film of the trooping of the colour, a Mickey Mouse cartoon, and the feature film, *The Man in the Mirror*, starring Edward Everett Horton and Genevieve Tobin; this also played for the remainder of the week. Much was made of the cinema's Holophone colour lighting, and Mirrorphonic talkie apparatus. During the mid 1930s most cinemas replaced the early sound reproduction equipment as the technology advanced. The Mirrorphonic, fitted at a number of the town's cinemas, was the most up-to-date; it was supplied by Western Electric, a leader in the field. The by now obligatory car park was also provided, and the building also housed a cafe, in which Saturday night dances were held; in its early days Ern Lockett and his band provided the music. The building was also equipped for use as a theatre, and was used by local operatic societies. Pantomimes became an annual feature from the late 1930s.

The cinema was owned by Esther Harriet Burns. Mrs. Burns started in the business in 1912, when she and her husband, James, opened the Electra cinema in Cheadle. Following James Burns' death in 1926, Esther continued to operate the Electra alone, and in 1934 opened the Forum in Wythenshawe in association with W. J. Davies. The Forum was also designed by Charles Hartley. However, eighteen months later, in April 1936, both cinemas were sold to the ABC circuit, and the proceeds used to build the Davenport.

The cinema prospered during the boom of the war years; it was run by Mrs. Burns, with the help of her son Cyril, and usually changed programmes twice weekly. In March 1954 a wide curved screen and stereophonic sound equipment were fitted, and the following month the cinema became the second in the town to present a Cinemascope film; this was *How to Marry a Millionaire*, starring Marilyn Monroe.

In September 1964 Mrs. Burns sold the cinema to Tatton Cinemas, who also ran the Tatton in Gatley, and the Savoy in Heaton Moor. The seating was by now reduced to 1707. Esther Burns was eighty-nine years old, and maintained an interest in the cinema from her nearby home until her death, four months short of her hundredth birthday, in February 1975.

In the month following the takeover the new proprietors reopened the cafe/restaurant which had been closed shortly before, and also began to close the cinema on Sunday in line with the policy of their other cinemas. The cafe was finally closed in the early 1970s, and in 1972 was converted into a second cinema; this was christened the Minor, and contained 180 "luxury armchairs". It was fully air conditioned, and was opened on Thursday, 21 December 1972, with the musical film *Oliver*.

In December 1970 the town was briefly without any of its four cinemas, with the Savoy, Essoldo and ABC all closed for alterations, and the Davenport closed for pantomime rehearsals.

The number of live shows presented at the Davenport increased under Tatton Cinemas, and though closed as a cinema on Sunday, live concerts remain a regular feature on that day. Pantomime is also a regular annual feature; the 1986 *Cinderella*, with Lewis Collins, was the theatre's 22nd such presentation. The Compton organ has also been in use recently, and Charles Brown began playing it at Friday night performances from August 1985. The cinema/theatre is one of the three remaining in the town, with the main auditorium now seating 1690. In early 1986 the front of the building underwent extensive alteration to give the theatre a more modern look.

Interior of Davenport Cinema 1937.

The Davenport Cinema, Buxton Road, in 1986.

Carlton, Essoldo, Classic, Cannon

The Arderne Cinema Co. Ltd. was incorporated in 1936 with a capital of £25,000. The company name was derived from the town house of the Arderne family in Underbank, which was then used by the company's bankers. The managing director was J. T. L. Mallard; his father-in-law, Enoch Edge, until his death in June 1938, served as Chairman. J. T. L. Mallard's involvement with the cinema trade had begun when he formed a company to take over the Palladium in 1933, and the success of this venture led to plans for the building of a new super cinema; the outcome of his plans was the Carlton, which opened on 28 July 1937. The Palladium passed to Richmond Cinemas, but the company acquired the Star, and Edgeley, from Elijah C. Aspden in 1937. In the following year a separate company was formed to take over the Grove cinema.

Mr. J. T. L. Mallard in 1937

The Carlton was designed by the Manchester firm of architects Drury and Gommersall. Joseph Gommersall was particularly well-known for the many cinemas he worked on in the Manchester area. The cinema was built on a site previously occupied by the Zion Church, and some old shops on Wellington Road South. It was largely the creation of J. T. L. Mallard, who, wherever possible, used local firms and suppliers in it's construction. He chose British sound and projection equipment supplied by British Talking Pictures Ltd.; this included the Truphonic sound system. The cinema included stage facilities, and a large orchestra pit, but no organ. It had seating for 1750. Originally there were separate entrances for the front and rear stalls. The cafe was entered from the front of the building, and a staircase leading down from the foyer. The cafe opened in July 1937, and in November an enclosed car park close to the Ritz cinema was opened with space for 500 cars.

The 300 guests present on opening night included the Mayor and Mayoress, and the Cotton Queen of Great Britain. The manager Albert "Mac" Parker had moved across from the Palladium. The programme: "opened with selections by the Northern Military Band, under the skilful conductorship of W. H. Ketchington. The band played delightfully and included the moving 'Poet and Peasant' selection, followed by Universal Talking News, Modern Tokyo (Traveltalk), *Mickey's Elephant*, *La Fiesta de Santa Barbara*, and an amusing musical production featuring Jack Buchanan, *This'll Make You Whistle*". Seat prices were 4d., 6d., 9d. and 1s. 0d. for matinees, 6d., 9d., 1s. 0d., 1s. 3d. and 1s. 6d. for weekday evenings and 9d., 1s. 0d., 1s. 6d. and 1s. 10d. for Saturdays and holidays.

Early programmes occasionally included live acts. One of these was Petulengro and his Romany Band and Dancers, who supported the film *Elephant Boy* in November 1937. Usually programmes consisted of one feature film supported by shorts, and often included a Disney cartoon. Successful early programmes included *Fire Over England*, and Errol Flynn in *The Charge of the Light Brigade* and *The Adventures of Robin Hood*. A stage prologue, *Birth of a Star*, arranged and created by Marjorie Knutton, was presented before the evening performances of *A Star in Born* in March 1938. The showing of this film also launched a publicity campaign offering a prize to the first baby born on the film's opening day. Sunday concerts presenting the bands of Jack Payne, Jack Hylton and Henry Hall played to full houses. In the early years of the war both

MANAGER TO YOU . . .

Dear Patrons,

As I write this brief message, expert craftsmen are putting the finishing touches to your new theatre, The Carlton. It has been a fascinating experience to see this lavishingly equipped edifice emerge from what we recall was formerly the site of an uninspiring group of old property. The familiar quotation, "He builded better than he knew," aptly expresses the completed work. For that reason my overwhelming pride in being privileged to hold the managerial position entrusted to me can well be imagined. And I am confident that similar feelings will be experienced by those hundreds of ardent cinema-goers who will make the Carlton their principle entertainment venue.

We have presented you with a theatre possessed of vivid beauty, charming to the eye, seductive in comfort and equipped with the best in modern science. The Carlton is surpassed by none. and brings to Stockport facilities hitherto enjoyed only in our few large cities.

To make this enterprise complete now demands an essential — pleasing entertainment. With the co-operation of my Directors, whose policy is to present only the best in screen programmes, I am able to announce that we have secured bookings which will substantiate this policy. It is with no desire to boast that I claim to have special qualifications for prescribing your entertainment. As manager of the Palladium, I have had ample opportunity of study in the matter of local preference.

Coming to Stockport in 1919 after serving in the Great War, I entered upon my career in cinema showmanship. Throughout those years I have made contact with a large proportion of the people in this district, and it is with considerable personal satisfaction that I now enjoy many pleasant friendships in my managerial capacity.

MAC PARKER.

May I now extend a very hearty invitation to all old and new friends to visit the Carlton regularly. I can promise you an interested welcome from

Yours very sincerely,
MAC PARKER,
Manager.

Albert "Mac" Parker in 1937.

Walt Disney's *Pinocchio* (1940), and Charlie Chaplin's *The Great Dictator* (1941), were retained for further weeks. In December 1940 the cinema ran *The Birth of a Baby*, passed by the local Watch Committee. Admission was only to persons over 18 years of age, and three separate matinees were reserved for ladies only, with all other performances open to mixed audiences.

In 1939 J. T. L. Mallard also formed Tegarn Cinemas to run the Palladium, and later the Wellington. In 1946 the Grove was sold to George S. Smith. In 1948 the two companies, Arderne and Tegarn, were taken over by the Essoldo group based in the North East, for a figure, "in excess of £100,000". A legal case concerning shareholder Catlow Greenhalgh, and his opposition to the takeover, dragged on until 1950. The companies retained their individual identity until the following year when they were absorbed into the Essoldo company. J. T. L. Mallard retired from the business affairs of the town to concentrate on running the Siddall ice cream company in Ashton-Under-Lyne, a company in which he had acquired an interest during the post war rationing period to ensure supplies for his cinemas. "Mac" Parker now became Essoldo's general manager in Stockport, controlling their five cinemas.

The Essoldo circuit was run from Newcastle upon Tyne by Sol. Sheckman who had started the company in the 1930s. By 1948 they controlled seventy cinemas nationwide, and at their peak in the 1950s would control almost 200. The company name was derived from the first letters of the Christian names of Scheckman, his wife Esther and daughter Dorothy. In April 1950 the Carlton was renamed the Essoldo.

In September 1950 it was reported that 24,000 people had seen *Treasure Island* during it's first weeks run, but the cinema's record for attendances was still held by *The Road To Morocco*. *Jolson Sings Again* also proved popular, and was retained for a further week in the same year. Mac Parker collapsed at the cinema in August 1953, and died later in hospital. He was fifty five years old. He was replaced, for a short time, by Joseph Michael Brooks who had also run the Reddish Essoldo. There were a number of managers in the 1950s and 1960s: including John Livingstone, Frank Page, Frank Seymour and Vincent O'Brien; the latter also came from the Essoldo, Reddish, in September 1963, but he collapsed and died at the cinema in January 1964.

In February 1954 over £8,000 worth of Cinemascope and Stereophonic sound equipment was fitted, and Monday 1 March saw the first Cinemascope film *The Robe* open at the cinema. It was held over for three weeks to be followed by the equally successful *How to Marry a Millionaire*. In April 1956 Davy Crockett, then a national craze, appeared at the cinema in the person of actor Fess Parker. The Two Eyes Coffee Bar opened briefly in the basement in 1958, and later that year the 21st anniversary celebrations were held. Prices by this time were 2s. 0d., 2s. 9d., 3s. 0d. and 3s. 6d. From November 1960 a number of Sunday evening pop concerts were held, featuring, among others, Adam Faith, Emile Ford and the Checkmates, The Shadows and John Leyton. In March that year *Gigi* had enjoyed a three week run at special prices ranging from 3s. 6d. to 7s. 6d., and in October the highest ever Sunday takings were recorded for Alfred Hitchcock's *Psycho*. The year 1961 brought Elvis Presley in *G.I. Blues*, *The Magnificent Seven*, *The Guns of Navarone* and Hayley Mills in *The Parent Trap*, all of which were retained. In August the Carlton Super Bingo Club opened in the basement. The following year *El Cid* was held over for three weeks, and the first James Bond film *Doctor No* for two weeks. By the time *The Longest Day* Played for three weeks in 1963 prices were 3s. 0d., 4s. 0d., 5s. 0d. and 6s. 0d.

In September 1970 the cinema was closed for renovation, and when it reopened on 17 June 1971 the building had been split into two. Essoldo 1 in the old stalls area, seating 522, and Essoldo 2 in the old circle area seating 325. Essoldo 1 was fitted with a 70 mm projector, and 6 track stereo sound. Essoldo 2 had a fully automatic projection system eliminating the need for reel changes. The conversion had cost £153,000. Essoldo 1 opened with *Anne of the Thousand Days*, with seats costing 60p; and Essoldo 2 presented *Soldier Blue*, with seats at the price of 50p.

In September 1971 Eric Sands, chief projectionist since opening, having started at the Palladium in 1929, retired. In March of the following year the cinema was taken over by the Classic chain, then owned by the Laurie Marsh Group, and renamed the Classic. Permission was granted for late night shows in 1977, but none were presented. In 1979 the Classic chain was taken over by Sir Lew Grade's Associated Communications Company, and in May 1982 the present owners, the Cannon Group, headed by Yoram Globus and Menachem Golan, took over. With the company's acquisition of the Star circuit in August 1985 it became the second largest cinema chain in the country with 216 screens in ninety five cinemas. In April 1986 the cinema's name was changed to the Cannon, and the following month the group took over Thorn EMI cinemas to become the largest cinema chain in the country.

The admission price of £1.80 has been held for both screens since about 1982, and recently some success has been achieved with a reduced price of £1.00 on Mondays and Thursdays. Successful films now play for longer runs, and 1985 saw large audiences for *Police Academy 2*, *Ghostbusters*, *Rambo*, and *From a View to a Kill;* all played for three weeks or more.

Interior of the Carlton Cinema, Wellington Road South, in 1937.

The Carlton Cinema, Wellington Road South, in 1937.

Ritz, ABC

During the 1930s the Union Cinema chain experienced rapid growth, and by 1937 had opened almost thirty new cinemas and taken over and modernised many more. The Rota was absorbed in 1936, and in 1937 construction started on a cinema in Stockport on what was known as the Town's Yard site. In September the financial organiser of the company, David Bernhard, died suddenly and, by the end of the year, Associated British Cinemas (ABC) had successfully taken control of the company.

The Ritz (a usual name for Union cinemas) was opened on Monday 3 January 1938, and by the end of the month was advertised as under the management of ABC. The cinema, standing on Duke Street, was the town's largest, seating 2343 on opening; there were 716 seats in the circle, and 1627 in the stalls. The first programme, playing to reported packed houses, presented Ronald Colman in *Lost Horizon*. The admission prices ranged from 6d. for stalls and 1s. 0d. for the circle at matinees, to 6d. and 1s. 0d. for stalls and 1s. 3d. and 1s. 6d. for the circle in the evening. The manager, T. Hellett, was described as having: "long experience with ABC". The building had been designed by architects Verity and Beverley, who also worked on a number of other Union cinemas. Also provided was a free car park for patrons. An unusual feature was the fitting of some seats with the Ardente system; this allowed deaf aids to be used by the hard of hearing. Also included was a Wurlitzer organ; it was played at the opening by Wilfred Southworth. Roy Bentley, a native of Cheadle Hulme, who had been played at Liverpool cinemas, was appointed resident organist at the end of January, but was replaced by Frederick Haig in June. Haig soon left to become a circuit organist for ABC, and in this capacity he frequently played at Stockport. The organ was removed from the building during the 1960s.

As the town's leading cinema the Ritz presented some of the year's big films, and early shows included *The Good Earth* and Laurel and Hardy in *Way Out West*. In November 1943 it presented the town's first run of *Gone With The Wind;* for two weeks the film was shown twice daily at 1.30 p.m. and 6.15 p.m., at special prices of 5s. 6d., 4s. 6d., 3s. 6d. and 2s. 9d. T. Hellett left in March 1939 to be replaced by W. F. Maxfield from the Plaza cinema; the latter left to join the forces in February 1941. Ernest Grant came from the Forum, Wythenshawe, to run the cinema, and he was followed by Douglas S. Baker in the mid 1940s. F. J. Burns was appointed manager in August 1948, and remained until his retirement in June 1953. One member of the staff who remained at the cinema from its opening until his retirement in the 1970s was Fred Sadler, the chief of staff, a well-known face to all the cinema's patrons.

In October 1946 the popular Saturday morning performance for the ABC Minors Club was started, and ran successfully until the late 1950s. The post war years saw a number of promotions: in 1950 there was a visit by Patricia Dainton, star of *The Dancing Years,* during the run of that film, and a beauty contest was held during the run of *Neptune's Daughter,* starring Esther Williams. Wilfred Lyons came from the Forum to become manager in 1953, and he was replaced by Eric Bailey in 1957. October 1953 saw the showing of the 3-D film *House of Wax,* with prices ranging from 2s. 3d. to 3s. 6d., and in the following January a widescreen was fitted ready for the screening of cinemascope films. In August 1956 Robby the Robot visited the cinema during the run of *Forbidden Planet.*

By the late 1950s the cinema was advertised as the ABC Ritz, but in December 1962 the neon sign at the front of the building was replaced, and the name officially became the ABC. Mike Ronan, from the ABC Wythenshawe, was appointed manager in 1968, and the following year reintroduced the ABC Minors which enjoyed some success for a short period. After a long takeover battle ABC finally became part of the EMI group in 1969. In November-December 1970 the cinema was closed for four weeks for extensive modernisation. An application made in May 1974 by Ladbrokes to use the building for bingo was rejected, but in July 1975 EMI announced that the cinema was for sale. A petition was raised by the staff of twelve to fight the closure, and in October the town council announced a plan to buy the building for use as a multi purpose leisure centre. The following month this plan was rejected, and in December EMI reported a sale to the London and Manchester Properties, who appeared to be more interested in the car park than the cinema. In January 1976 Mike Ronan moved on to the ABC Deansgate in Manchester, and it was reported that: "the post (of manager) would not be filled in the near future". The same month saw the largest audiences for years at the cinema during the run of *Jaws*. The proposed sale fell through, and in April 1977 EMI announced that they had decided not to sell.

One year later in April 1978 the cinema was leased to G. A. Young Enterprises based in Berwick-on-Tweed. Major Geoffrey Young ran three other cinemas, and two hotels. By this time the seating had been reduced to 1750, but only the circle was used as the size of the audience warranted no other arrangements. The cinema was again named the Ritz. During this period the cinema seemed run down, and a pale reflection of its former grand self. The sound reproduction was particularly poor. The Tatton group attempted to buy the cinema for a number of years, but to no avail, and the end came on 11 December 1982. The closure was blamed on rising costs, falling admissions and the rise of the home video recorder. The building remained empty, but in December 1985 a sign appeared outside offering it for sale as a "development site". The seating was removed in February 1986. In January 1987 a sign indicated that it had been sold, and work began on the demolition of the building to make way for a car park in May 1987.

The Ritz Cinema in May 1960.

County, Essoldo

Jackson and Newport Ltd. the company run by Arthur and Harry Jackson and Edward Newport, were involved in running four cinemas in the Reddish area. They first took over the Pavilion at the Bull's Head in 1932, renaming it the Embassy, built the Rota after the loss by fire of the Embassy, ran the Bijou with Frank Donaldson after the Rota was sold to ABC in 1936, and finally built the new County cinema on the corner of Gorton Road and Priory Lane. The company also ran cinemas in Stretford, Little Lever and later Prestwich.

The County, designed by Henry Elder of the Manchester firm of architects Roberts, Wood and Elder, was opened on 28 March 1938. It was a small super cinema in line with the standards of the day, providing a car park at the rear of the cinema and including shops in the building. Seating was provided for 1300; 1050 in the stalls and 250 in the balcony. The opening week featured Binkie Stuart, "Britain's Baby Star", in *The Rose of Tralee* for three days; this was followed by Errol Flynn in *The Prince and the Pauper*. The manager, Joseph Michael Brooks, who was to stay until 1953, had moved over from the next-door Bijou cinema and managed the two cinema until the Bijou was closed. As a local cinema the County usually showed the second run of films after their appearance at the town centre cinemas. Following the war, and the reduction in the number of films available, small independent cinemas suffered badly; and the County would often programme re-issues, and newer B-films, particularly westerns. For this reason the County, along with many other small cinemas, became known as the "Ranchhouse"; with frequent jokes replacing the cinema car park with a hitching rail for horses.

In August 1950 the cinema became the ninetieth to join the Essoldo group, their sixth in the town. In September 1951 the name was officially changed to the Essoldo, but it was still known locally as the County for many years. In 1953, following the death of "Mac" Parker, Joseph Brooks was appointed to the post of Essoldo's general manager in Stockport, and Vincent O'Brien, from the group's Wellington cinema, became manager of the County. In September 1963 he was appointed manager of the Essoldo Stockport, and Reg Vivante became the cinema's final manager.

Permission for a change of use to Bingo was granted in November 1966, but it was not until 15 March 1969 that the cinema was closed. At first it was announced that this was for "extensive redecoration", but it was later admitted that the building was being converted to use as a bingo hall at a cost of £40,000. The final programme was a double bill: *The Magnificent Seven*, and the sequel *Return of the Seven*. By the time of closure the seating had been reduced to 1080. In common with many ex-cinemas it was found that one night's receipts from bingo were often more than week's takings from the showing of films. The building, again named the County, remains in use as a bingo hall.

The County Cinema, Reddish, in 1987. Now a Bingo Hall, the building is largely unchanged on the outside.

Empress

The Empress Cinema, Manchester Road, nearing completion in 1939.

The last cinema to be built in the town, The Empress, on Manchester Road, was opened on Saturday 6 May 1939. The opening night audience was offered *The Scarlet Pimpernel*, starring Leslie Howard and Merle Oberon, at prices ranging from 6d. to 1s. 6d.. The following Monday and the next two days, *The Goldwyn Follies* was screened at the cinema.

The proposal to build the cinema had met with considerable opposition from local residents, who had forwarded a 300 signature petition to the town council. The site had previously been occupied by the Ash Farmhouse, at which the promotor of the cinema, Harry Hitchen, son of a local councillor, had spent his early life with his grandparents. The original plans called for a 200 table whist hall, a dance hall for 500, a nursery in which patrons could leave their children while visiting the cinema, and six full size tennis courts. In the event the ballroom, and the cinema seating 1400, 700 in the stalls and 700 in the balcony, were the only parts realised. The car park offered space for 1000 cars. The architect, J. B. Cutts, was also managing director of the company.

The opening was perfomed by the Mayor, Alderman T. E. Hunt, and the programme also included Alice Swindells, the All-British Accordian Champion of 1936-37. The manager, A. E. Barron, had started as a pianist at a cinema in St. Helens, before being appointed manager at the age of twenty. He had spent the last eleven years as a cinema manager in Nottinghamshire, and was well-known for playing piano with local dance-bands.

In December 1939 "Wally" Baker, ex-manager of the Palladium, returned to the town, becoming manager of the Empress until January 1942. With his usual flair for showmanship he began a number of promotions; these included a pancake day treat in 1940, when 500 children were given a free show. Other events included a Free French dance; he also introduced Harry Korris and Robbie Vincent, stars of the radio programme, Happidrome, at a Grand Cinema Carnival Ball in 1941. October 1940 saw the cinema advertising its: "Basement Air Raid Shelter—heated, ventilated, seats, music, refreshments".

After resigning from the cinema "Wally"

Baker was appointed manager of the recently reopened Hippodrome, now a live theatre, where he stayed until May 1943. He then left the town again, first to Southport for the summer season, and later as office manager for Columbia Pictures in Liverpool and Manchester. In October 1949 Baker went missing from his home in Denby Lane, Heaton Chapel, for six days, but was found dead in a field in Derbyshire.

In August 1943 the cinema changed hands. The new company included directors Thomas H. Claughton and John L. Claughton, who were also involved in the management of the Curzon cinema in Offerton. Harry Hampson, ex-manager of the Wellington, was appointed manager in 1945. He introduced "Discoveries", a local talent show he organised, and also lectured at local schools on "The Influence of Cinema in Modern Life". He left the cinema in 1950. In July 1956 the cinema joined the Plaza as part of the G. B. Snape circuit, with L. Kelly acting as manager. The Empress was closed on 18 April 1959, showing Jerry Lewis in *Rock-a-Bye Baby*. By the time the cinema was closed the seating had been reduced to 1129. The ballroom was to remain open.

On 9 December 1959 the Empress Cabaret Club, run by Keith Marsden, an ex-Manchester City footballer, opened in the part of the building previously used as a cinema. In 1961 parts of the building were used as the Flamingo Coffee Jive Club, and the Empress Bingo club. The Empress Club closed as the result of a fire in May 1967, and remained closed until reopened in December 1968 as the Poco-a-Poco Club and Casino. Later the club changed hands, and became known as Chesters. The building was finally demolished in June 1987, and a public house built on the site.

Cinemas in the District Around Stockport

In 1974 local government reorganisation created the Metropolitan Borough of Stockport, and added a number of surrounding urban district councils to the old county borough. The following list covers the cinemas that served these areas.

	Opened	Closed
Bredbury and Romiley		
Palace (Bredbury)	1914 1971	1961 1972
Savoy (Romiley)	1934	1963
Forum (Romiley)	1971	Open
Cheadle and Gatley		
Electra (Cheadle)	1912	1963
Cheadle Hulme Cinema	1922	1930
Elysian (Cheadle Hulme)	1930	1974
Tatton (Gatley)	1937	Open
Hazel Grove and Bramhall		
Village Hall (Bramhall)	1912	1912
Grove/Cosy Grove (Hazel Grove)	1913	1960
Tudor (Bramhall)	1935	1958
Marcliff/Warwick (Hazel Grove)	1937	1954
Marple		
Shepley Hall	1911	1915
Gem	1915	1931
Regent	1932	Open

Bredbury and Romiley

The first cinematograph licence I have traced was one granted to the Public Hall Co. Ltd., in February 1914, for their building in Beech Lane, Romiley. Part of the premises were sublet to the Liberal Club. The first cinema to open was the Bredbury Picture Palace, on Mill Lane, which opened in May 1914. It was built for the Palace (Bredbury) Co. Ltd. based in Union Street, Stockport, and was later run by Grenville Stansfield, son of Hyde cinema pioneer Wilbraham Stansfield. Constructed mostly of wood and corrugated iron, the paybox was in the porch and the shape of the building lead to its local nick-name "The Barn". Like many outlying areas there was either no public supply of electricity, or a very unreliable one. One witness commented: "when a tram went past the lights went out!" For this reason many cinemas, including the Bredbury Picture Palace, had their own generator. Prices were in line with standards of the day, 2d., 4d. and 6d., with a special children's matinee on Saturday for 1d., 2d. and 3d. There was seating for about 500, and one show nightly at 7.30 p.m., except for Saturday when there were performances at 6.50 p.m. and 8.50 p.m. A unique feature of the cinema was the "Stereoscopic Screen", of which there were, reportedly, only two more in the world, both in America.

The cinema gradually came to be known as the Palace. During the 1920s a pianist at the cinema was Napoleon Bird, who ran music shops in Chestergate and Lord Street. He held the record for nonstop piano playing of three days and nights. On Thursday evenings a dance band would be in attendance to play the latest songs, while the words were projected onto the screen. Talkies were introduced in March 1931.

On 22 September 1950 the Palace became the Cinema Playhouse, with the Bredbury Players opening in the play *The Paragon*. This policy of mixing films and live performances continued until the building was closed on 16 May 1953. It reopened on

The Palace Cinema, Bredbury, 1987, now a snooker hall.

Monday 25 May 1953 under new management, now dedicated solely to films, and the name reverted to the Palace two weeks later. The cinema was now part of the Tatton group run by Nash Eaton, who instituted extensive alterations and modernisation; the work included an extension to the building. In September 1961 the U.D.C. granted permission for a change of use to a bingo hall, and this opened for business on Friday 1 December 1961.

During the late 1960s there were rumours that the Bingo Hall would close, and finally the Palace reopened as a cinema on 12 August 1971. The first programme was *Those Magnificent Men in Their Flying Machines*, and there was one admission price of 30p. (15p. for children). The proprietor, Clifford Henstock, had made extensive alterations over the previous four months, and eventually hoped to "twin" the cinema. However by March 1972 manager Harry Johnson was complaining of the competition from the recently opened Forum, run by the UDC, and at the end of May it was announced that the cinema was to close and return to bingo. The building is now in use as a snooker centre.

The Savoy cinema, on the corner of Sandy Lane, Romiley, was officially opened by the Chairman of the company, Major Raymond Hill on Saturday 6 October 1934. The building, designed by architect Albert Winstanley, of Manchester, seated 300 in the circle and 700 in the stalls, and included a cafe

The Savoy Cinema, Romiley, about 1951. The crowd is watching a display by the fire brigade.

The Forum, Romiley, in 1987.

on the first floor looking out onto Sandy Lane: this was later converted into offices. There was also a free car park. The managing director and cinema manager was Charles T. Woolley, a twenty-four year old rugby enthusiast, who had worked for a Northern cinema circuit. Other directors included a Manchester solicitor, J. H. Hancock, and Frederick S. Eaton, who would later be involved with the Curzon cinemas in Offerton and Flixton. Admission prices were 8d., 1s. 0d., 1s. 3d. and 1s. 6d., and the first public performance on Monday 8 October presented George Raft and Carole Lombard in *Bolero*.

Charles H. B. Dowding, who had recently been at the Deansgate cinema, Manchester, took over as manager in March 1937. During the Second World War, Joseph A. Scoggins, the cinema's projectionist, took over the post, while his wife became projectionist. In early 1952 the cinema was taken over by Sidney Wild, who also ran the New Prince's in Stalybridge and the Rialto in Irlam. Wild had worked at Paramount for fifteen years in Manchester, and during the war worked with Sidney Bernstein, the founder of Granada Television. Other shareholders included W. T. Kelley, of Leigh, and George S. Smith, who ran two cinemas in the Stockport area.

The cinema included an orchestra pit, and primitive dressing rooms under the stage. Live shows were presented, and included offerings by the Romiley Amateur Operatic Society. The area only permited six-day cinema opening, but Sunday bingo sessions took place from 1962. The cinema closed on Saturday 19 October 1963, and the last film was Cecil B. DeMille's *Samson and Delilah.* The building reopened on 24 October as a Bingo Hall, and continued to be run by the Wild Leisure Group until the end of March 1986 when it was closed. The building is for sale, and it is likely that a supermarket will appear on the site.

The Forum in the centre of Romiley, while not a full-time cinema, does occasionally present films. It was opened in December 1971, and officially opened by Princess Margaret on 11 May 1972. Run at first by the Bredbury and Romiley U.D.C., and now by the Leisure Services Division of Stockport M.B.C., the Forum's first film presentation was *My Fair Lady* in March 1972.

Cheadle and Gatley

The Electra on High Street, Cheadle, was opened on 26 August 1912. The original cinema was a primitive building with no balcony. Much of its seating for 900 was on wooden forms, at prices of 6d. and 9d., with the last three rows of tip-up seats at 1s. 0d. The proprietor, James Burns, was involved in the cotton trade, and had got the idea of opening a cinema from relatives in the USA. His son Cyril worked at the cinema from the age of seventeen, and returned after service in the forces during the First World War. In 1915 alterations were carried out; they included a new front to the building, and moving the operating box upstairs.

Late in 1923 the cinema was closed for large-scale reconstruction. The new Electra, a more solid and comfortable building, opened on 28 February 1924. James Burns died in May 1926, and the running of the cinema was taken over by his widow, Esther Harriet Burns. Mrs. Burns was a strong-willed and resourceful woman, who now moved into a flat she had built above the cinema. The Electra was one of the first cinemas in the area to install Western Electric talking picture apparatus, and Al Johnson in *The Singing Fool* opened on 30 October 1929.

In 1934 Mrs. Burns, in conjunction with Stockport councillor W. J. Davies, built the Forum cinema in Wythenshawe, but less than two years later, in April 1936, both the Electra and the Forum were sold to the ABC circuit. Early in 1954 the cinema was leased by ABC to the G. B. Snape circuit, which controlled the Plaza cinema in Stockport. In 1960 a rumour that the cinema was to be demolished, and a supermarket built on the site, was denied. In mid 1961 there was much outcry over Sunday bingo sessions held at the cinema, which was still restricted to a six-day opening policy by the U.D.C. Following much criticism from local church groups the bingo sessions ended after a few weeks.

The Electra Cinema, Cheadle High Street, about 1930.

ABC sought outline planning permission in June 1962 for the use of the site as a supermarket, and on 9 November 1963, when the Snape circuit's lease expired, the cinema was closed. The Electra was demolished in August 1965, and a supermarket now stands in its place.

The Cheadle Hulme Cinema, on Mellor Road, opened on Wednesday 25 October 1922. Private shows were held for the first three days, and the cinema opened to the public on Saturday 28 October showing the film *Midsummer Madness*. Largely constructed of corrugated iron and wood, the cinema seated 300: "in comfortable chairs of the latest design". The opening, presided over by the Chairman of the controlling company, W. H. Tutton, was described as: "bright and attractive, and much enhanced by the vocal efforts of Mr. D. Birtles, a brilliant baritone, and the delightful strains of a bijou band".

The cinema was never a great success, and soon settled into a routine of one performance nightly, plus a children's matinee on Saturday. Even a large scale and successful film such as *Ben Hur* could not fill the cinema, and the average weekly audience was under 1000. It remained open because the running costs were low, a reported £5 per week. One patron described how: "the village postmistress, Mrs. Ridgeway, used to play the piano after taking the money at the cash desk". Another pianist at the cinema was Thomas Evans, ex-musical director of Stockport's Cinema Theatre. After an unsuccessful attempt to prevent the building of the nearby Elysian cinema, the Cheadle Hulme Cinema, still showing silent films, found it hard to compete with talking pictures and closed soon after the Elysian opened in November 1930.

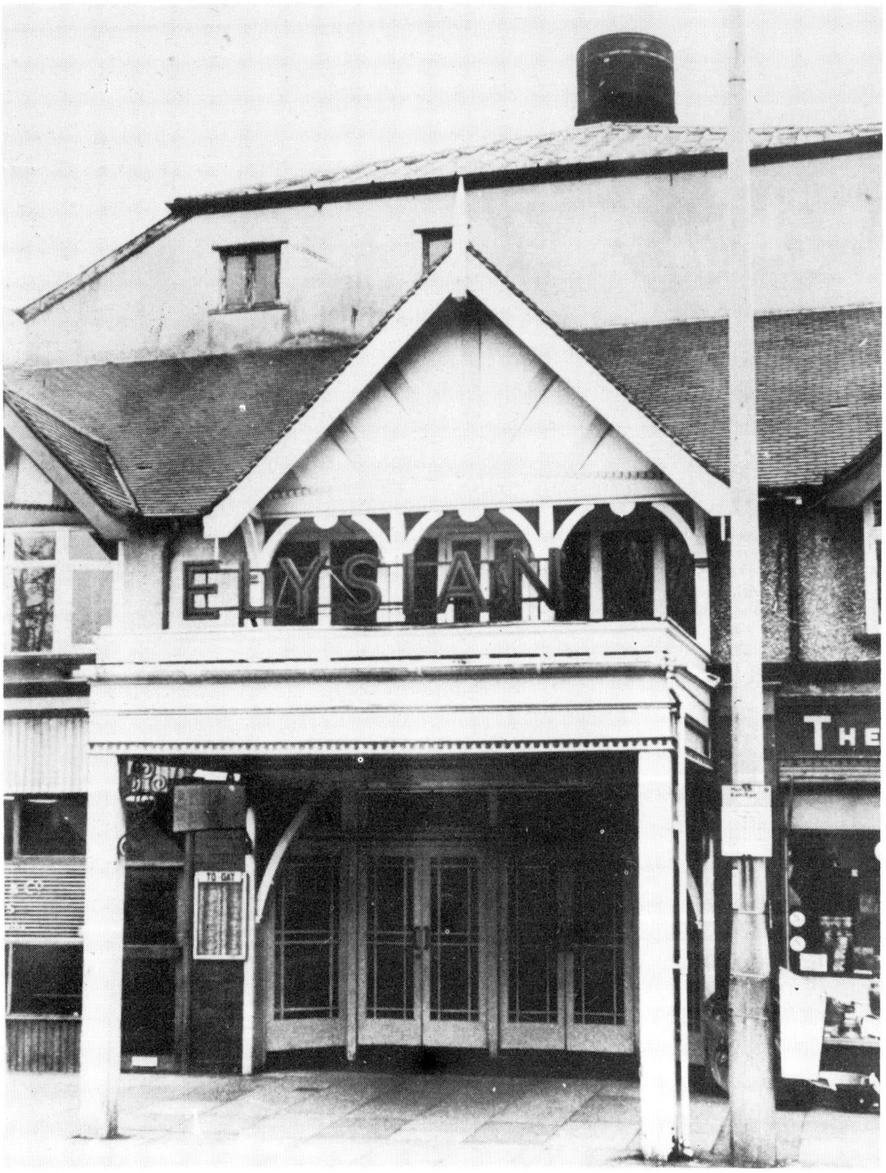

The Elysian Cinema, Cheadle Hulme, shortly after closure in 1974.

The Tatton Cinema, Gatley, in 1987.

Cheadle Hulme's second cinema, the Elysian on Station Road, was built by local builder W. W. Stansby, who was also the cinema's first proprietor. The formal opening, on Saturday 22 November 1930, presented a number of variety acts, and the film *Behind the Curtain*, to an invited audience. The first public performances, the following Monday, presented *Rio Rita* at prices of 9d., 1s. 0d. and 1s. 3d. (1s. 6d. on Saturday). The cinema, designed by Stockport architect Herbert McLellan, seated 900 and included a free car park for patrons. The space above the proscenium was decorated with a seascape by Mr. F. Garner, of Stockport. J. W. Griffiths served as general manager, and the cinema manager was Tom Robinson.

The cinema was closed for almost two weeks in February 1931, when a fire destroyed the stage and fittings. W. W. Stansby also built and ran the Rex cinema in Wilmslow, which he opened on 15 October 1936. Plans for a third cinema in Gatley, to be called the Curzon, were scrapped when it was beaten by Nash Eaton's Tatton cinema. In April 1956 W. W. Stansby announced his intention to sell the Elysian, and in October it was taken over by Dennis C. Walls, a local councillor, who also ran cinemas in Derby, Preston and Rusholme. A former general manager of the Emery circuit, he had been president of the national Cinematograph Exhibitors Association in the 1940s.

The final proprietors were Alfred Lees, who had run the Coronation cinema in Northenden, and his son-in-law Tom Blakeley, a film producer and son of John E. Blakeley, founder of the Manchester Film Studios on Dickinson Road. The cinema closed on 2 March 1974, and the final film was *The Day of the Jackal*. It was purchased by the London based firm of property developers, the London and Manchester Securities, who had been buying up shops on Station Road. The building is now used as a supermarket.

The Tatton cinema, on Gatley Road, was opened on Thursday 14 October 1937. It was run by Ernest Nash Eaton, who had started in the cinema business in 1910, and had been involved in the building of many cinemas in the Manchester area. The remainder of the directors of the controlling company were members of the Blackburn family, who ran Thomas Blackburn and Son of Preston, a firm which supplied steelwork used in the construction of cinemas. The firm's band was on hand for the cinema's opening, and the film shown was *Jungle Princess* with Dorothy Lamour. The building, designed by architects J. B. Teasdale and M. C. Sunter of Manchester, also included a restaurant, a stage 18′ deep and six dressing rooms. Western Electric Mirrorphonic sound equipment was installed, and seating provided for 900 in the stalls and 300 in the balcony.

The company took over the Savoy in Heaton Moor in 1948, and the Palace in Bredbury in 1953. Nash Eaton died in May 1957, aged seventy five, and Vera Edge, who had worked at the Tatton since it opened, took over as proprietor. The company is now run by her son, Jack Edge.

On 4 February 1971 the minor cinema opened in the area previously occupied by the restaurant. Built at a cost of £16,000, with seating for 100, it was the first cinema in the country to have fully operational rear projection. The minor's first programme was *Airport*, with all seats at 10s. 0d. The large auditorium was now called the major. On 17 November 1975 the major closed, and reopened as two auditoria on 28 November 1975; the new major was created out of the old stalls area, and the new minor from the old circle area. The old minor then became known as the mini. With its three screens the Tatton is now the most successful cinema in the group, and regarded as one of the most successful cinemas in the North West.

A further cinema was planned for the area in 1939, and architect J. L. Edwards drew up plans for the Cheadle Development Co. Ltd.; the building was to include a cinema, shops and flats on the site of the Old Rectory, Wilmslow Road. Demolition began on Monday 21 August 1939, but the plans were stopped by the outbreak of World War Two.

Hazel Grove and Bramhall

The area's first cinema proved to be shortlived. In March 1912 the Village Hall on Ack Lane, Bramhall, opened as a Picture Palace. Run by George Herbert Henshall, it was initially only licenced to open from 8 p.m. to 10 p.m., but in April the hours were extended to allow matinees to be held starting at 2 p.m. The proceeds of the performance held on Tuesday 23 April were donated to the Titanic Relief Fund, and the programme included a special film entitled *Icebergs in the Atlantic*. The cinema closed for the summer in May, and did not reopen.

The Grove Picture Palace on Commercial Road, Hazel Grove, opened on 3 February 1913. Local firms were given preference in the construction and fitting of the building, with George Oldham, of Commercial Road, serving as the building contractor, and Charles Robert Locke, of Stockport, as architect. Seating about 500, the cinema was run by the Grove Cinema Co. Ltd., with Ernald Edward Allison, ex-manager of Stockport's Cinema Theatre, acting as manager. Initially there were two separate performances nightly, at 7 p.m. and 9 p.m., with matinees at 3 p.m. on Wednesday and Saturday, and separate performances on Saturday at 6.30 p.m. and 8.45 p.m. However, local complaints that the earlier show was too early, and the later show too late, lead to continuous performances between 7 p.m. and 10.30 p.m. being introduced from 17 February.

During the summer of 1916 the cinema was closed for extensive decoration and painting, and closed again on 2 June 1917. When it reopened on 10 September 1917 there were new proprietors, namely Thorne and Marples, with J. W. Marples serving as resident manager. In March 1929 the cinema again changed hands, and was taken over by Mr. and Mrs. P. and H. Hall; they installed sound equipment in the following year, and the first talkie programme, *The Donovan Affair*, opened on Monday 10 March 1930. During the 1930s Thomas Knott, ex-proprietor of Stockport's Vernon cinema, became resident manager until the cinema again changed hands in May 1938. J. T. L. Mallard, managing director of the Arderne cinema company, formed a new company, the Grove Cinema (Stockport) Ltd., to run the cinema. By this time the cinema had a free car park. The company's other director was Gifford Hallam, an electrical engineer of Marple Road, who had also been a director of Stockport's Palladium cinema earlier in the 1930s. In early September 1938, the box office was besieged by patrons eager to see *Scarface;* this was billed as: "the film Stockport banned".

Pensioners leaving the Grove Cinema, Hazel Grove, after seeing a free film show to celebrate the Coronation of George VI in May 1937. The photograph was made from a cine film taken on the occasion.

The final proprietor George S. Smith, who also ran the King's cinema in Stockport, took over in November 1946 and renamed the cinema the Cosy Grove. He, together with A. M. Patterson, submitted a proposal to the U.D.C. in October 1960 calling for the conversion of the building into a club, and admitted that the cinema was losing money. In November the proposal was rejected, and the cinema closed soon after. In June 1961 a further proposal to use the site for a supermarket was also rejected. Finally it was announced in October 1961 that the site would be used for a new postal delivery and sorting office, and the cinema was demolished shortly after.

Bramhall's new cinema opened on 31 March 1935. The Tudor had roads on three sides: Woodford Road, Birch Road and Maple Road. It was built by contractors William Briggs of Stockport, and seated 550 in the balcony and 700 in the stalls. The building also included a cafe, which opened shortly after the cinema, three living apartments, shops and a car park with 1000 places. Admission prices

Drawing of the Tudor Cinema, Bramhall, in 1935.

Cover of the Tudor Cinema programme May 1957.

were 6d, 1s. 0d. and 1s. 6d. for the stalls, and 1s. 6d. for the balcony. The first public performance presented Clark Gable and Claudette Colbert in *It Happened One Night*.

The company which controlled the cinema, Bramhall Tudor Cinema Proprietors Ltd., had as directors: General Manager George Davies, who came from five years service at the Paramount (now Odeon), Manchester; the cinema's architect George Clayton; Arthur Derbyshire; and Catlow Greenhalgh. Greenhalgh came from a Burnley family who had run a preserves factory in Reddish, and his brother John had been Mayor of Stockport during 1925-26. In the 1940s he would become involved with the Arderne cinema company.

The cinema had a number of interesting features. The interior was described as: "cream coloured walls relieved with stained oak panelling, massive oak pillars and cross-beams giving an impression of real English solidarity and genuineness". The walls were also decorated with pictures of Henry VIII and his wives. There was also a: "Press Room . . . which will be equipped with stationery for those, who for some reason or other, can dispose of correspondence arrears or lounge for a while rather than break into the middle of the star film."

William Revill, a member of the family which ran the Theatre Royal in Stockport, became manager in late 1935. There were also a number of stage presentations including in July 1935: "Eva Greenhalgh of BBC fame in a spectacular prologue to *One Night of Love*", and in April 1938 Violet Carson, "the famous BBC artist". The cinema's early days gave rise to a number of law suits arising from disputes between the directors, and they culminated in George Clayton appearing in the bankruptcy court in 1939. In 1937 Alfred Snape, managing director of the Plaza cinema in Stockport, bought a half interest in the company, and also became managing director of the Tudor.

The cinema became part of the James Brennan circuit, based in Manchester, in

January 1947, and from the 1 January 1950 became home for Frank H. Fortescue's Number One Repertory Theatre Company. In April 1952 there was a reversion to films, and in December the cinema again changed hands. It was taken over by Dennis C. Walls. In January 1953 repertory theatre began again with the Tudor Players, under General Manager, and Producer in residence, Bernard Graham. Bad weather was blamed for poor attendances and, after six weeks, Dennis C. Walls pulled out and the Brennan circuit took over again. Films were quickly reinstated, beginning on 30 March 1953.

In January 1955 the Brennan circuit's lease ran out, and the cinema was closed. It reopened on 2 January 1956, showing *The Student Prince* in Cinemascope; it was under the management of the original company, now controlled by Catlow Greenhalgh who lived in Bournemouth. He died in a Manchester nursing home in October 1956, aged eighty five, and the running of the cinema was taken over by trustees. In September 1958 they announced that the cinema would be put up for sale by auction in October, but agreed to continue to show films until the building was sold. However the cinema was withdrawn from the auction when the bidding reached only £8,000. It closed on Wednesday 15 October 1958. The final programme was a double bill of *Bitter Victory*, and *Decision at Sundown*. At the time of closure the seating capacity was 903. In September 1959 the building was purchased by the U.D.C. for £1,500, and in February 1961 pulled down to make way for the supermarket which now stands on the site.

Hazel Grove's second cinema was the Marcliff, on Macclesfield Road; it was opened on Tuesday 12 October 1937. The opening ceremony was performed by Miss Vera Greenwood, Cotton Queen of Great Britain, and the first film was *Secret Interlude*, starring Robert Taylor and Loretta Young. There were 764 seats. Construction had been the work of Stockport builder Clifford Ogle, who was also the proprietor. His other concerns included the Woodbank open air swimming pool, and two cinemas in Knutsford. The name Marcliff was derived from the names of his two children, Margaret and Clifford. The architect, Herbert McLellan, who had also designed the Elysian cinema, Cheadle Hulme, included an auditorium of the "stadium" type, with the balconet being at a slightly higher level than the rear stall seats. There was a free car park, and the cinema was fitted with R.C.A.'s "high fidelity" sound system. The manager, Reg Egerton, had formerly been with cinemas in Llandudno and Wrexham.

In October 1949 the cinema was taken over by Warwick Cinemas (Timperley) Ltd., who also ran cinemas in Hale, Middleton, Gorton, Sale and Wilmslow. The cinema was renamed the Warwick in January 1950. A poll held in Hazel Grove in November 1952 resulted in a decision against Sunday opening, and the area continued a six day opening policy. By the time the Warwick closed on 11 April 1954 programmes were changed three times a week. The last film shown was *Fort Algiers*, starring Yvonne de Carlo.

The building reopened on Monday 19 April 1954 as the home of the Frank H. Fortescue Repertory Company. The opening show was the musical *Me and My Girl*, and the following year newcomer Peter Adamson joined the company. The Warwick closed as a repertory theatre on the 19 January 1957. The building is still standing, and is now used by a car hire firm.

The Marcliff Cinema, Hazel Grove, October 1937.

Marple

Marple's first regular film shows were held at the Shepley Hall, now the Conservative Club, on Church Lane. A cinematograph licence was granted to James Rolmaz in July 1911, and the hall was later run by Henry Lawrence. In August 1915 Lawrence moved from the Shepley Hall to new premises in Church Lane, which he called the Gem cinema. The Shepley Hall was later used for occasional film shows. By all accounts the Gem was a primitive, mostly wooden structure, with the seating consisting largely of wooden benches. The Gem survived until the arrival of talking pictures under a number of proprietors. These included Messrs. Morris and Ryden of Hollins Lane, Marple, with N. Cooper acting as resident manager, and Walter Stott, a well known figure in Manchester cinema circles.

In February 1931, when an application was made to extend the opening hours from 10.30 p.m. to 10.45 p.m., the Gem was described as shabby by the police, and the clerk to the magistrates warned that unless the cinema was put into a presentable condition the licence might be in jeopardy. In October Harold Wright, the then licencee, applied for a dramatic, music and dancing licence in respect of the cinema. "The Talkies have come into vogue", he said, "and as the place is not large enough to install a talkie apparatus, we intend to run performances by dramatic societies and concert parties". The new policy began on Monday 20 October 1931. The building was later used as a meeting hall.

Early in 1932 a plan was approved for the conversion of the Union Rooms, and three adjoining houses on Stockport Road into a cinema. The Union Rooms had been built by Thomas Carver, owner of Hollins Mill in Marple, as a chapel, coffee room, library and reading room for the destitute. Later it was

The Regent Cinema, Marple, in 1986.

used by the Congregational Chapel. The original plans, drawn up by William Thornley (architect of the Plaza, Stockport) for Walter Stott, entailed clearing the site and building an entirely new cinema to be called the Rialto. In the end the cinema, the Regent, was a conversion of the existing buildings. It was designed by architect R. N. Sampson, of Sheffield, for the Marple Cinema Co. Ltd. The managing director, Ernest S. Allen, was based in Sheffield. Fitted with British Thompson Houston sound equipment, the cinema seated about 500. The same company had also taken over the Arts Theatre in New Mills in 1930, and reopened it as a cinema early in 1931.

The Regent survived into the 1960s in a poor state of repair; it was run by manager Ray Taylor, a well-known local character, and later, in its final days, by manager, projectionist, boilerman and caretaker Lawrence Corbett. It was closed on 3 August 1968, and put up for sale. In December an application was made to the U.D.C. for the use of the building as a bingo hall, but this was refused. The U.D.C. then planned to issue a compulsory purchase order for the building, but it was finally reopened as the New Regent cinema in June 1969, by David Lillis.

David Lillis had experience of cinema management with the ABC circuit, and with the help of his father, almost completely renovated the cinema. The circle seating was replaced with Pulman seats, new stalls seats installed and the interior redecorated and recarpeted. The cinema now seats 252. Until four years ago they also ran a twin cinema in Matlock, but now concentrate on running the Regent. In line with national trends attendances have been up during the last two years, but some films can still perform poorly. The Regent has excellent projection and sound facilities and general standards matching the best in the area.